From an old knuckle dragging target in *Under Fire*. I wish there had been something like this for my time 40 years ago, but as they said in the first *Gumball Rally* movie while ripping away the rear view mirror, "What is behind us is not important!" The past is past.

Paul Lee, Executive Director for Fellowship of Christian Peace Officers (FCPO)

*Under Fire* is a timely and practical testimony that promises to awaken talking points in relationships targeted for ruin. Kristi's experience and tender approach welcomes weary, wounded, warrior-families to experience healing, and hope in what seems darkest moments within Law Enforcement, today.

Jack Crans, Pennsylvania State Police, Chaplain

As a wife of a deputy, this is a must read. *Under Fire* will guide you on improving your communication with your officer, and give support to overcome the many stresses we encounter as the wife of an officer.

Christie Cooper - Wife of Deputy Matt Cooper; 1st Grade Teacher

# UNDER FIRE

## *Marriage Through the Eyes of a Cop's Wife*

### By Kristi Neace

International Standard Book Number: 978-1512190571

*Cover image:* Rick Berk, Rick Berk Photography, www.rickberk.com. Used by permission.


*Within the pages of this book, "officer" will (for the majority) be referred to as "he/him" and "spouse" as "she/her". This is in no way intended to overlook or devalue the importance of our female officers, but simply describes the majority of situations I encounter, and better communicates what I have experienced.

# *Love*

Love is a friendship that has caught fire.

It is quiet understanding, mutual confidence, sharing and forgiving.

It is loyalty through good and bad.

It settles for less than perfection,

and makes allowances for human weakness.

Love is content with the present.

It hopes for the future and it doesn't brood over the past.

It's the day-in and day-out chronicle of irritations, problems,

compromises, small disappointments, big victories,

and working toward common goals.

If you have love in your life,

it can make up for a great many things you lack.

If you don't have it, no matter what else there is,

it is not enough, so search for it, ask God for it, and share it!

- Author Unknown

# Contents

# Dedication

To all those who have struggled and overcome...you are true heroes.

To Rick - my partner in life, thanks for sticking with me all these years. I love you!

# Special Thank You

A special thank you goes out to Mark Mynheir for graciously volunteering to edit this book in its entirety. Your expertise was much appreciated!

Introduction


Every love story has a beginning. Two people meet, fall in love and live happily ever after...right? Unfortunately, it's not always that easy. Anytime a couple of completely unique personalities are meshed together there is bound to be conflict. They learn quickly what makes their love interest tick, or what causes them the most anxiety and pain. Add to that mix the stresses of law enforcement life, and things can spin out of control.

Two souls who were once total strangers, acting and reacting with their best foot forward, are confronted with the problems associated with sharing that life together. Their true personalities, hurts, opposing desires, and life baggage bubble to the surface. Inevitably, both become vulnerable to emotion that sweeps over them like a rushing wave. Certain expectations arise and undergird everything they believe marriage ought to be, like a tidal wave those expectations come crashing down with reality. Somehow life has a way of interrupting the bliss, and expectations begin to go unmet. Finances, children, in-laws, careers and a host of other issues bombard the union with destructive force, and...if the pair does not discover the glue that can hold them together, the marriage will often fail.

I understand these things...I've lived it. *We've* lived it. That's why I share stress factors and other parasites that can attack a marriage, along with ways to combat them, on the pages of this book. Perhaps, just maybe, our personal journey and understanding can give you a renewed hope and a firm footing into this thing called marriage. Law enforcement life is hard. From swing shifts to missed holidays and special occasions, to lack of communication, Rick and I have worked through these common job-related issues and so many more. It is my hope that what we've learned can help guide you along, providing encouragement to make it work.

# Chapter 1

*"A Police wife is* a woman who is married to a man who is 'married' to his job, his partner, and his badge." - Unknown

The Early Days

Rick and I began our journey together in high school. We were inseparable and enjoyed every moment we could steal away for just the two of us. He had big plans to go into law enforcement after graduation, and I had big plans to follow him wherever he went. No agenda. No desire to do anything else besides to embark on the quickest professional school I could get through. And so that's what we did. I graduated in January of my senior year of high school and began Metro Business College shortly after; Rick worked at an electric company and hardware store until he turned 21 and could then enter police academy.

Life was grand. We married in July of 1988, two months after my high school graduation with not a penny to our name, and a baby on the way. Our faith? It was not strong, though it had been engrained into both of our lives from infancy. We chose to live for the day and for each other, not for God. We would soon reap the consequences of our youthful immaturity and spiritual neglect. Our marriage would not survive…or would it?

The Change

I hear so often the dreaded phrase from many poor law enforcement wives or girlfriends, "He's changed." Yes, it's true, he *will* change and not usually for the better, at least not at first. Within months of graduation from the academy, my officer morphed from a carefree, fun-loving personality to someone who was somewhat withdrawn, suspicious and cold. It's as if a light switch had been turned off and his personality had become programmed to handle the most evil of circumstances.

In reality, the serious demeanor, suspicious nature, and acute awareness of their surroundings are necessary survival tactics in order to carry on in a civilized manner after a continual assault on their emotion and psyche. You or I would be no different if put in their shoes. No human in their right mind with any ounce of compassion could walk away from a grisly murder scene or tragic car accident time after horrific time without completely losing their mind, especially, if he or she didn't somehow learn to box it up and place it in the attic of their thought life. Yet, I didn't understand that, and it made me crazy trying to figure out what I had done to warrant this new behavior and his changed attitude.

These "Do not open" boxes – compressed memories of those things which no-one should have to experience, stack up over the years one on top of another, crowding out everything and everyone until at some point, the officer is forced to deal with the clutter. By then, however, the damage of harboring feelings such as anger toward a child molester, deep sadness at the tragic scene of a young teenager killed in a car accident, or the blaming of self for not being able to save a hostage victim, is done and oftentimes, their marriage or relationship is over. The enemy has won another round in destroying the family unit.

Honestly speaking, not every officer becomes that detached, but the majority does. Not every officer shuts down when he or she comes home, but most do. If you are an exception to that rule, then celebrate! You've been given a tremendous gift, and one that should not be taken for granted. However, for the rest of us out there, we understand the loneliness that comes with all those "Do not open" boxes and it can be maddening. The truth of the matter is, that even in the best of circumstances all officers are changed by the job, though some more drastic than others, and unfortunately, those changes can negatively affect a marriage.

Circles

The first years of our marriage, Rick not only worked as a police officer with all the crazy swing shifts and sleepless nights, but also volunteered as a firefighter for a local department, and helped out at the EOC (Emergency Operations Center) within our town. Needless to say, he was absent from the home a large majority of our early marriage.

By this time, I was busy with two little ones and a full-time job. There were no spare moments for friendships other than the ones I had at work, and definitely not much left over for us as a couple. Date nights were pretty non-existent as we struggled to make ends meet and find time for our own interests. Our stress levels were at an all-time high, and he and I were pretty much just co-existing in the same home – he in his circle and me in mine.

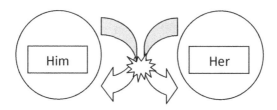

If you look at the example above, this pretty much summed up our life, and is very similar to what happens in most law enforcement marriages. The officer, we'll call him "He," is living out of one circle going in one direction, working and trying to balance home and work responsibility, as well as dealing with stress and issues on the job.

The wife or "She," is moving in the opposite direction taking care of her responsibilities in the home, the children, her husband, holding down a job or working as a stay-at-home mom, and dealing with her own set of stresses.

If they don't have something to glue them together in the middle of their circles, all they really do is rub up against each other causing friction and a whole host of conflict. If the two of them are never completely fastened as one unit, they'll often fling off into opposite directions; a typical event in law enforcement relationships that we see over and over and over.

### The Glue

As for Rick and me, we were spinning out of control, literally. Our marriage was on a fast track to divorce, and I was the biggest promoter for calling it quits. Did I believe in divorce? No, not really, but I couldn't see any other way. There were no "feelings" of love anymore, and it had become more of a burden than a blessing. I remember numerous heated arguments where blame and insults were hurled back and forth with me making it plain that divorce was high on my agenda. I was ready to move on. Find someone new; someone who would be there for me. I was tired of being a single parent and feeling less than important in my husband's life. Thankfully there was one aggravating deterrent which kept us hanging in there…finances. We were in such financial disarray neither of us could afford an attorney! We were stuck together, whether we liked it or not, and forced to find some type of glue to start putting the pieces back in place.

I'd like to tell you it was easy, but it wasn't. I'd like to say that all went smoothly from this point on out, but it didn't. It took work…first by figuring out that the glue we needed was a committed relationship with God, but also by putting the other's needs before our own, finding ways to help and support each other, and to carve out time for just the two of us. There were also lots of tears, prayers and humbling on both parts. Both of us had to lay aside our selfishness and refocus on the "we" aspect of the relationship. Each had to give 100% in order to get the same out of it; hard work, but so worth it. We both had to embrace not only who we were as a couple, but also the *One* who had brought us together in the first place. We needed God to fix our seemingly hopeless situation and become the foundation on which everything else would rest upon.

Over the last several years, the two of us have had the pleasure of talking with many couples on the verge of divorce. It has become such an easy solution to a burdening problem. Society tells us that if it doesn't work, throw it out. Everything and everyone is disposable. Yet, that's not the best solution, nor the perfect plan for our lives. Marriage can work and can become a solid foundation not only for our family, but generations to come. We must break the cycle plaguing our society, and get back to the original formation of the family unit – a sacred covenant that God designed between a man and a woman for life. If He designed marriage, then we can believe He is able to heal it and rebuild it.

On more than one occasion, Rick and I have witnessed individuals surrender to the fact that they can't fix it. At that moment of brokenness and in their despair, often they look up out of sheer desperation and realize that it's not all about them. Once that light bulb goes off and they are positioned in the right direction, these couples begin to reap blessings of fulfillment and joy within their marital relationship. Take for example Mike and Courtney:

> Mike and Courtney, a law enforcement couple we casually knew, began having extreme marital problems.
>
> Mike was not meeting Courtney's needs, would come home and absorb himself in his own thoughts and agenda, and completely neglect hers and those of their children.
>
> After trying unsuccessfully to reroute his attitudes and actions, Courtney found comfort in the companionship of another man. Fights erupted. On more than one occasion the local police (not his department) were called to domestic

altercations. Neither would leave, but both were miserable.

Hurtful words and accusations were slung out across media sites where the world had a front seat to their pain. His superiors strongly urged him to leave as things escalated, and threats to his job were issued if the charades continued.

Finally, the last straw came when Courtney moved out of the house. To Rick and me, things seemed hopeless, but both he and I continued to urge the husband to fight for his marriage; she was not on talking terms.

Months into the breakdown, a miracle began to take root. First one, then the other slowly turned towards God and ignored the counsel of the world. Both began attending church and a local bible study. Feelings of love for the other were returning, and eventually, Mike and Courtney came back together as husband and wife.

Today, their love is stronger than ever. They found their glue in God, and He began to repair the brokenness in their marriage. They are now becoming the complete unit they had committed to be in the beginning.

When our friends found their "glue," and placed God in the center of their marriage, the pair became one force moving in the same direction and not against one another. Though it may seem simple, many either do not take the time, or simply ignore the fact that godly glue is the substance all marriages need for success and harmony. Without it, a marriage is on shaky and unstable ground.

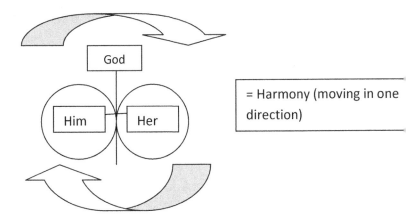

For Rick and me, once we both began to put God first allowing Him to fix us together as a unit, the condition of our marriage began to change for the better. That doesn't mean that we've always agreed or seen eye to eye on things, but it does mean that our level of commitment is such that no matter what we face, we hit it head on together.

So, let me ask you, how would you describe your relationship with your spouse at this point? Do you feel as if it is under fire or is your marriage safely covered from the enemy – bullet proof?

Regardless of where you are, I hope that something within the pages of this book speaks to your heart and helps to build that fortification around your family unit.

## Let's Talk

1. What qualities and characteristics first attracted you to your spouse?
2. Before you married, what was your view on marriage?
3. Did you and your spouse live together? If so, do you think it strengthened or stressed your relationship? How did it affect your relationship with God?
4. What is one area in your life that if changed, could better your relationship with your spouse?
5. What is your opinion of the circle factors that Kristi listed? Can you relate?

**Project:**

Find some creative ways to show your spouse how much he or she means to you this week. Leave encouraging notes in their pocket or purse, draw a big heart on the bathroom mirror with the words "I love you!" inside it, plan out an evening ahead of time full of surprises (flowers, borrowed or rented sports car, favorite restaurant, a scenic overlook with a romantic picnic, etc.).

Take pictures of the day/night and put them in a special frame in your house to remember.

## Chapter 2

*"It's been one of those days! I haven't been this sick in a LONG time and husband is on night shift with no end in sight. The kids are driving me nuts and I'm 5 hours away from family. I'm just feeling so sick, overwhelmed and exhausted. Lord, please give me strength to get through this day!!"*

It is no secret that law enforcement life is stressful. However, in addition to the stresses of the job, a lot of couples face these things alone without family or close friends who can or will step in and offer encouragement. Let me just say, you're not alone. Many, many folks are having the same struggles you are, and better yet, a large majority of those have found a way to make it work. Over time, you will too.

Stress Factors in Marriage

Let's look specifically at some things that can cause stress within a law enforcement/first responder marriage.

Perusing through an endless amount of internet statistics, I found that a number of these sites indicate anywhere from 65-80% divorce rate, though others argue that it is not that high. So why are there claims of such high marital unrest? Because there is a war on marriage collectively right now by the culture, the world and Satan. Divorce has become an easy alternative to difficult situations. Husbands and wives are seemingly "falling out love" with the other person and simply walking away leaving an aftermath of destruction. If the problem is not divorce, then it is simply a lack of commitment and the couple has chosen to just live together rather than "be all in."

When we enter marriage, there are certain expectations which naturally exist in all of us. It's as if we almost subconsciously assume that this person whom we love, is now going to make us happy and fulfill all our hopes and dreams. Right? Not so fast.

In our early marriage, I remember thinking, "Okay…here is this guy who is going to love me no matter what, spend time with me and fill me with such happiness." I later discovered what a foolish thought and unfair burden I had placed on his shoulders. True, he loved me, but inevitably that love would be challenged at times, especially when I was being unlovable. Though he may (or may not) have wanted to spend every waking moment with me, it was not feasibly possible. There would be many days and nights I would find myself alone.  In those times I was given a choice to either allow bitterness and resentment to creep in, or find ways to occupy my time allowing myself to feel like a contributor to something worthwhile, until we could find time to reconnect as a couple.  In my case, I opened the door for resentment to fester without even realizing it.

Through the years, though our marriage has ultimately brought much joy, there have also been times when it has caused heartache and pain.  We are human, and are going to fail one another at some point.  Simply put, a husband or wife *cannot* and *will not* be able to completely fulfill or meet every need you or I may have.  It is unfair to put such an unrealistic responsibility on their shoulders.

So what are some of the stress factors and reactions that can throw a wrench in our happy law enforcement wedded bliss?  Let's take a look at some below:


Officer

Poor diet

Lack of sleep

Financial deficits

Rotating shift work

Overall stress of the job

Job politics

Balance of responsibility

PTSD (Post Traumatic Stress Disorder)

Emotional shutdown

Exclusiveness


Spouse

Loneliness

Isolation

Financial deficits

Anxiety/fear

Loss of identity (particularly if wife is a stay-at-home mom)

Feeling disconnected/excluded

Overwhelmed (responsibility)

Disappointment

Balance (home, work, husband, kids, etc.)


As you can see, "the job" produces specific stress factors within a LE (law enforcement) relationship. Though other "civilian" marriages may experience similar issues, for the most part, they are unique to those whose spouse has a job of this nature.

Not only are there things which mentally and physically challenge the officer, but there are also factors affecting the spouse either in relation to what her partner is dealing with or as a direct result from the nature of the job. Let's examine a few of them a little closer.


**The Officer:**

Poor Diet/Lack of Sleep

How often has your officer sat down to lunch or dinner only to be called right back out, leaving his plate half finished? They're always on the go and rarely have the time to enjoy a well-balanced meal. Officers tend to grab what they can when they can, so most of the time it consists of fast food, high sugary intake, and zero nutritional value. A consistent diet like this can contribute to obesity, potential diabetes, high blood pressure, heart attack, etc. When he's not eating properly, it can cause him to be irritable and have a lack of concentration.

To top it off, their sleep pattern is routinely interrupted thereby slowing down their metabolism and causing their minds to become foggy and easily distracted. These factors alone are a recipe for disaster not only on the job, but in the home as well. For those dealing with swing shift schedules, bodies adapt to one shift only to be interrupted and replaced by another. Days off likely consist of either staying up late watching movies due to sleeplessness, or attempting to sleep while it's daylight and with more activity in the home. Their bodies have no way of coming down off the high they've been on, thus it often causes tempers to flair and words to come across hateful, snippy and cutting.

For Rick and me, one solution to the diet issue is the daily routine of juicing. Though it's not for everybody, this is one way we - especially him, can get quick nutrition that is easily portable and able to be taken in the car. Not only have we felt the health benefits of this process, but have also noticed some weight loss and greater energy level.

As far as the sleeping habits, I try to be more understanding and allow him to take naps on his days off, not seeing it as "laziness" as I once did, but now understanding that his body and mind are physically exhausted and need that extra boost. We try to maintain a routine schedule when he is off and get to bed at a decent time.

Also, something as simple as a leisurely stroll around the neighborhood, or even sitting out by the fire pit can help ease the stresses and cause the body to relax.

A verse that comes to mind when dealing with the stresses of this job is Matthew 11:28, which says, *"Come to me, all you who are weary and burdened, and I will give you rest."*

Now that's something you can take to the bank.

Financial Difficulties/Deficits

Financial strain and politics within a department can also cause an officer stress and frustration. All too familiar headlines like the following are plaguing our officers and their families:

*Detroit Police Officers Hit with Pay Cuts*

*State Trooper Forced to Collect ROADKILL to Feed His Family Due to Salary Freeze*

*Program Threatens Texas Police-Fire Pension Fund*

Pressures of budget cuts within the department can create great stress for an officer trying to figure out how to meet the growing demands of a family. Then on top, if he must work a second job in order to make ends meet, an officer will absorb more pressure and physical exhaustion within an already stressful situation.

I remember back in 1996 after we first moved to the St. Louis area. Rick was working full-time at his department, and part-time as a bank security guard just to pay the bills. Reflecting on those days, I realize he was burning the candle at both ends, but at the time it was the only way we could keep our nose above water. Could we have done without the newer SUV, the vacations and the swimming pool? Certainly. It would have been a wiser decision to forego those things and learn to live within our means and lessen the burden placed on him from those financial demands. The extra toys and wants paved the way to added stress and debt that both he and I would work to pay off over a long period of years, plus it opened up opportunity for tempers to be short and actions to not be quite as loving as they should have been. Definitely a learning experience.

Three and a half years ago, Rick and I went through the Dave Ramsey, Financial Peace program. We were amazed at the amount of money we were spending without even realizing it.

Things as simple as quick snacks and meals he was grabbing on the go, added up to over $200 per month. After making a list of all our bills and income, we chose to make drastic changes to our spending habits in order to pull us out of the debt tank.

First of all, Rick would take snacks and meals from home. That meant I would need to start preparing dinners in the evenings instead of the usual take-out. I learned to get pretty creative with the crock pot. This is where Pinterest recipes came in handy.

We also developed an envelope system where we allocated funds for expenses not automatically withdrawn from our account. Things such as groceries, clothing allowance, kids' school expenditures, fun money, etc. It was simply amazing to see the amounts of money grow instead of wondering where it all went!

It comes as no surprise that the old saying, *Dishonest money dwindles away, but he who gathers money little by little makes it grow,* makes a whole lot of sense.

## Overall Job Stress

Unfortunately, law enforcement today is so far removed from years past when there was still a level of respect towards officers and the badge they represent. The stress that these brave men and women face on a daily basis has escalated from not only dealing with the horrors of a depraved generation, but now an ever-increasing voice of resistance, hatred and persecution from those they have sworn to serve and protect.

This constant negativity and threatening, mob-like mentality has a way of escalating the level of stress, and gives way to previous uncharacteristic behaviors such as: hesitancy to act and react when placed in a threatening situation, lack of empathy, increased cynicism - "us against them" mentality, and deep-seated depression.

Any one of these behaviors can and will eventually filter down on the marriage and cause tension and strife between an officer and his or her spouse.

Take for instance the situation in Ferguson, Missouri in 2014. When Michael Brown was shot and killed by Officer Darren Wilson, riots ensued and the community was rocked by fits of aggression and violence.

Day and night for weeks, officers endured physical and verbal assault, as well as emotional and mental attacks not only by those protesting, but by the media, government officials and even Hollywood elites.

Conversations that my husband and I had with officers in Ferguson as well as many of those standing on the front lines from other departments, described a hellish nightmare that forced their stress levels almost to the breaking point. Many went days without sleep; weeks without days off to rest and reconnect with their spouses and children at home, and a number of them had to relocate their families for safety reasons, creating a whole host of other issues and stress factors.

The stresses of policing are under-emphasized and overlooked. If not properly dealt with, these things can play a major role in the dismantling of an officer's marriage and possibly his or her life.

Emotional Shutdown/Exclusiveness

Emotional shutdown is another issue that often arises in a law enforcement marriage. Each shift our officers deal with people and their problems, rarely catching a glimpse of anything positive. When duty is over and all senses are on an emotional overload, the best coping mechanism is to completely crash or shut down. This can cause a gradual communication breakdown between husband and wife/officer and spouse at what should be a reconnection time. Hear what one police wife said recently:

> *He comes home and all he wants to do is*
> *play video games or watch TV.*
> *Conversation between the two of us is*
> *almost non-existent.*

He's not emotionally or mentally ready to re-engage in family matters, create small talk, nor make decisions, even if it is something as simple as deciding on where or what to eat for dinner. The wife sees this indecisiveness or lack of interaction as a lack of interest in her, leaving her feeling unloved, or as if she's done something to warrant this behavior. What it really means is that the officer is in need of time to "defragment" or wind down before he can rejoin the rest of the family. Our minds have a way of compartmentalizing situations we've seen, feelings we've felt, etc. Therefore, after being on a high for so long, it is crucial to be able to place all that mental and emotional energy into their proper compartments as a coping mechanism.

With that said, however, it is extremely important that officers realize the need from their spouse to reconnect and rejoin the family unit after a period of defragmentation, in order to keep the circles flowing in the same direction.

> *She doesn't understand that when I walk in the door from a long shift, that is not the time to quiz me about the bad accident I just left from or the situation at the neighbor's house. I haven't had time to process it myself. Let me unwind and then I'll be ready to talk at a later time.*

Exclusiveness is another form of coping or protection of one's self that law enforcement couples often deal with. Officers tend to be exclusive, in that they will often retreat away from social gatherings with "civilians" and either stay to themselves or migrate around other officers who understand their way of thinking. Many times, officers will even turn away from their spouse and turn towards their co-workers because of a *she just wouldn't understand*, or *I need to protect her* mentality. Yet, this is the farthest thing from the truth.

I often give this scenario when speaking to cops about their spouse:

> Imagine that you get a call to respond to a person holed up in a home with a possible hostage situation. You are not told whether or not the area around the home is secure, if the perpetrator is a man or a woman, if they have a history of violence, if he or she is armed, or if there are more than one hostage. This scenario without the facts could be deadly. You are now walking into a potentially volatile situation blindfolded and unable to fully evaluate the circumstances at hand.

Now take that scenario and liken it to your spouse. If you never tell her anything about what you do, or give her insight into things you are dealing with, then she is walking through the relationship blindfolded without the ability to discern or adequately prepare. You may be right about her lack of understanding, but that's because you haven't shared any information with her.

Naturally, due to the complexity and sensitive nature of law enforcement, there are things the officer will be unable to share or divulge, but when possible, if he can open up about his job and stresses he faces, then the relationship will be on a much more solid footing.

Share with your spouse the good things that you do. Was there someone you were able to help or assist in some way? Take them down to the station and let them see where you work and become familiar with those you work with, or if allowed, ask them to join you on a ride-along.

If you were involved in some type of critical incident, understand that your spouse will probably find out through social media or others. With technology the way it is, I have heard of wives hearing that their husband was involved in a shooting ever before he had a chance to call her. Open up with what you can as soon as you can, so that she hears things from your perspective rather than those with half the truth or pure speculation.

Information when handled correctly is powerfully effective within a marriage. So I encourage you to make use of it.

**The Wife:**

Loneliness/Isolation

Wives of officers are subject to feelings of loneliness, disappointment and isolation. With their husbands often working long, unpredictable hours, many are left alone to care for the children and hold down the home front.

In our marriage, I often felt as if I was a single parent having to make important decisions or handle the majority of the parenting aspect on my own. Though I relish in the fact that I'm an independent personality type, I did come from a home where my father took care of everything. When it came to car problems, my dad fixed it. When water leaked under the door in the basement, my dad swept it up and fixed the door. When a storm approached, he was there to ride it out with us. Yet being married to a cop, this hasn't always been the case. More often than not and to no fault of my husband, I was the one to drop the car off for repairs, sweep the water, or hunker down with the kids in the basement. That was and is the reality of law enforcement life.

Recalling one particularly stressful evening, I remember when one of our children decided to display his pre-teen independence. Of course, dad was at work, and I was extremely tired and not in any mood to corral this young buck. So, in my frustration I found myself in the middle of a shouting match, resulting in hurt feelings on both ends, and an adolescent on the run. After a couple of hours and dark setting in, I called my husband in an anxious panic. Our son had not returned home, and I had no idea even where to look. Because Rick was tied up on calls, another officer was sent to scour the countryside looking for our lost little lamb. Eventually, he was found sitting at Wal-Mart a couple miles down the road, stubbornly waiting the situation out.

It's at times like this that we as wives want to pull out our hair. I remember thinking, *why can't I have a husband with a normal 8-5:00 job that is home in the evenings to help me? I didn't sign up to be a single parent!*

Loneliness and even resentment can set in especially if there is no family close by, or friends who understand your husband's position, and who can encourage you that it *will* be okay and you *will* get through these tough moments.

Disappointment

Then there is the matter of missed birthdays, school plays, baseball games, holiday festivities, etc. When we get married, it's easy to assume that those special moments will be shared with the one we love. However, when you are married to an officer, it's those memorable events which seem to take the most hits, often leaving wives feeling disappointed and even angry over the unpredictability of their husband's job. Let me share with you one police wife's frustrations as she tried to work through a scheduling conflict:

> *My husband is an SRO. This Wednesday is the last day of school for our district, and as of now he has yet to be given his summer assignment which starts on Thursday. I am total Type-A, and feel I can't plan much beyond Wednesday without knowing his schedule first. If I start penciling in "to-do" items on the calendar, sure as the world it will not work with his assignment. The really irritating part is that last week a memo went out requiring a 15 day notice to request time off for vacation or holiday. Ugh! Beyond frustrated!*

Over the years, Rick and I came to the understanding that he would be at events and activities when he could possibly be there, but there would be times when I would have to accept and be okay with his absence. Flexibility is key. I've learned to go on to activities that I want to go to such as church, sports games, family/friend gatherings and women's events which, in the long run, actually help pass the time and offer a sense of belonging, instead of me just sitting around dwelling on the fact that he's not there. Also, vacations were always decided at the beginning of the year, so they could be "penciled in" on the work calendar before it filled up with other requests for time off. Knowing that family time was coming was always a help in keeping my frustrations in check.

Anxiety/Fear

Anxiety is another issue hidden within the recesses of our minds. Though these thoughts may not display themselves every time he walks out the door or calls to say he's in the middle of a "bad situation," they are there regardless, and oftentimes find their way to the forefront of our mind when we least expect them to. *What if he doesn't come home? What if I get that knock on the door? How would I handle it?* Or even this one...*What would I wear if I was called to the hospital in the middle of the night!* These thoughts are a very real concern and can cause bouts of fear or apprehension. Below is one wife's post displaying some very real fears:

> *Hubby's SWAT team got called out last night for a domestic call of a barricaded subject with a hostage. Immediately, I felt a pit in my stomach, so got up and began to pray. I heard them call out rescue for a medic. My nerves were about shot at that*

*point. Awhile later my cell phone rang, and*
*I nearly killed myself stumbling to get to the*
*phone. It was my husband saying they*
*made entry into the house and the subject*
*was in custody. He had a few minor cuts*
*and scrapes from the scuffle, but was okay,*
*thank God! This is the part the public*
*doesn't understand – what we go through at*
*home.*

Often when I'm speaking to officers and their spouses, this is something I discuss. Our officers can easily forget this side of law enforcement stress on their significant other. They often get caught up in the moment of what's going on, having first-hand knowledge of a situation, yet their spouse at home may possibly be catching bits and pieces through news media, social media, or other sources of information without having the whole picture.

At that moment, the mind has a way of playing tricks on the thought life. Fear and anxiety can become a very real emotion and cause feelings of stress in the spouse. This is why it is crucial for an officer to touch base with his wife as soon as he can, as well as to help her understand the nature of his job. She, on the other hand, must realize that there will be moments when he simply cannot phone or text because of the circumstances. Sit tight, pray, and wait for his response. And remember…you are never alone. God assures us in Joshua 1:9 with these words, *"Have I not commanded you? Be strong and courageous. Do not be frightened, and do not be dismayed, for the Lord your God is with you wherever you go."* ESV

## Loss of Identity

I've heard numerous wives who stay at home to care for their children say, "I'm nothing but a mom." What a sad statement! Women who stay home to raise up their little ones have one of the most thankless, tiring jobs there is. Yet, for those married to law enforcement officers, these women often feel as if their identity becomes Officer _____'s wife or the children's mother.

I stayed home for a little over a year and a half after we moved to the St. Louis area. At the time, I remember struggling to figure out who *I* was. Rick was the one with the flashy badge, name tag, and standing in the community. We couldn't go anywhere, including out of state, that he didn't know someone or be recognized because of his job. I would politely smile while trying to blend into the background feeling less than important, though that was farthest from the truth.

It finally dawned on me that I needed to re-discover who I was...to look for ways to carve out my own path in life. So, I began classes at our local community college, wrote and published a few poetry pieces, and took on our women's ministry group at church. These things helped me acquire an identity of being more than just "Rick's wife" and my kids' mom, though those roles were very important.

## Feeling Disconnected

Women are relational, meaning we want and need reconnection after a period of separation with those we care about. Friends who haven't seen each other in a long time can pick up right where they left off. Mothers and college-attending daughters can sit up all night talking about everything from shoes to boys. Likewise, wives need reconnection with their husbands when there has been a period of separation from a job, training or something else. But with that said, we need to remember to give our officer time to defragment when he re-enters the home. Hitting him up at the door with the bad report card, the latest car issue or that your mother is coming to stay for a few days will probably not bode well. Give him time to physically and mentally switch from work to home before re-engaging.

As I stated before, officers come home and shut down because of the mental and emotional high they've been on. Wives, on the other hand, desire reconnection. If communication does not take place, she is going to feel insecure and disconnected within the relationship, which may lead to nagging and complaining and finally escalation of the situation. Husbands love your wives by opening up and sharing some of your day with her. Instead of being harsh or unresponsive, show her attention. Take a little time to listen to frustrations she may have or highlights of her day. Put your arm around her or hold her hand when you sit down together on the sofa. Pour her a cup of coffee or make her favorite milkshake. It's the little things that go a long way, and may benefit you in the end. Wink.

With these and many other contributing stress factors within a law enforcement marriage, many couples simply do not make it. A number of them are unwilling to spend the necessary effort to work through the struggles they are facing, and more-than-likely have not found the glue that will hold them together.

With that said, however, it *can* work and your marriage *can* thrive. I've witnessed it *and* lived it. With a little hard work, a lot of prayer and a good support system, we can change the statistics. I truly believe that!

## Let's Talk

1. From the above list of stress factors, what is the one that you most struggle with if any?
2. Think of ways you and your spouse try to reconnect as a couple. Are there other things you could be doing to help strengthen the relationship?
3. How are your finances? Do you stick to a budget or do you struggle with extra, unnecessary purchases?
4. What types of things are you involved in that help build your own identity?

**Project:**

Make an "I love you because" list. Both you and your spouse list on separate sheets of paper what you love about the other person. It may be simple like "I love the way you make my pancakes," or "I love the way you know what I'm thinking even if I don't voice it."

Put the lists in envelopes and tuck them away for those moments when you are frustrated and distant from one another. Get them out and remind yourself about why you love your mate. ☺

# Chapter 3

*"Anybody else get bad insomnia when their hubby works overnights? It's after midnight here and I can't sleep!!!"*

## Communication, Communication, Communication

Back in the day when Rick went into the academy, it was three…long…weeks! Every time I tell that, I get a room full of snickers and gasps. Yes, looking back on it now I see how blessed we were that it wasn't longer. Yet at the time, it was *three weeks* of separation that we had never had before as a couple, *three weeks* of no daddy around, *three weeks* of complete single parenting and decision making that made me question, *Did I really sign up for this?*

Today, training for our officers is more high-tech and likely takes in the better part of a year up front. Its nature is to stay up to speed in order to keep the badge one step ahead of the ever changing methods of the bad guys out there on the street.

Academy instructors are diligent to prepare our officers the techniques to survive, how to fight, how to shoot, how to drive, but what they so often fail to teach them is how to *thrive* in their marriage.

As I began building my presentation for Badge of Hope Ministries, I scoured the internet for statistics on law enforcement marriage and how the stresses affect the relationships at home. Here's what I found:

- Depending on which site you look at, a number of them estimate that the LE divorce rate is anywhere from 65-80%, and is claimed to be the highest of all professions. (*Firefighters also claim to have the highest divorce rate)

- 75% of LE spouses deal with stress that is a direct result of the officer's police work (Matthews, 2011)

- 90% of couples dealing with stress say that communication issues are a big concern (Matthews, Law Enforcement Stress and Marriage, 2011)

- Domestic violence is 2 to 4 times more common in police families than in the general population. In two separate studies, 40% of police officers self-report that they have used violence against their domestic partners within the last year. (Brannan, 2001)

- Police officers going through a divorce are 5 times more likely to commit suicide than that of an officer in a stable marriage! (http://www.heavybadge.com/efstress.htm)

- 85% of first responders and 35% of dispatchers experience some symptoms of PTSD. (Michaels)

- "In a 20-25 year career span it is not particularly unusual for an officer to go through 6-8 marriages." (Haines, 2003)

Scary figures, aren't they? As I made my way through the list, I was in awe of what ripple effects these job-related stresses can create and filter down onto wives, children, significant others, etc. I had a light bulb moment! Most of our early marital conflicts could directly be related to the stresses we experienced as a law enforcement couple. I did not understand it at the time, but looking back on some of our battles, it finally dawned on me that we were not ordinary. This job was not ordinary. He was stressed. I was stressed. Both of us were spinning in our separate circles, and we had no glue to hold us together. Depression set in. Neither of us was happy and both were looking for some type of solution. Divorce seemed like an easy out, though thankfully we fought for what was important instead of becoming another statistic. And through all of it, we were not alone. Scores of law enforcement couples across the country were and still are dealing with some of the very same scenarios and feelings of isolation.

Listen to my friend Karen, describe her uphill battle to save her marriage:

> I truly do not know where to begin. I've been an LEO wife for 23 years and thought we were doing everything right. We were living the charmed life. He worked crazy hours, shift work, court, etc., and I stayed home and took care of the children, and tried to make our home a haven.
>
> I had never been too caught up in the Law Enforcement world. We had a few friends from the department, but we lived a distance away, so getting together with them wasn't always an option.
>
> In 23 years we experienced life's ups and downs like any married couple. Throughout those years I noticed his faith wavering, but he would always make a "turnaround". I chalked it up to being part of the job.
>
> We went to church as a family, prayed, did church activities; me somehow thinking that would be enough. Then about 3 years ago it seemed to get worse. I don't know if you believe in attacks from the evil one, but after surviving what we went through, I no longer have any doubts. It caused me to pray like

never before…. "Bring him home! Use whatever means necessary."

Things just didn't seem right. For the first time, I could not put my finger on it. He was pulling away and I could not get him to talk to me at all. It seemed as though we were living different lives. I did what I needed to do for the kids and the house and the family, while he was working more and more. He was angry, mean and said VERY hurtful things. I was in tears all of the time because the man I so dearly loved wasn't happy and I knew it.

Crying out, I begged him to tell me what I could do. I didn't want to be the reason for his unhappiness. When he wouldn't answer, I believed the lie that it was me.

I prayed and through prayer I came across the *Love Dare* which I dove into like my life depended on it.

The ironic thing is my personality dictated a very different approach. Anyone who knows me understands my natural response would have been to say, "Well, then get out!" The Lord was definitely at work here.

I thought that if I became a better wife, mother, housekeeper, it would repair our marriage. There was more overtime and court than ever before, but no overtime pay. When I questioned him it was met with excuses like, "Someone new started in payroll, and they don't know what they are doing."

Then he was picking fights with me every chance he got. I couldn't do anything right. I was also pretty sick at the time. The doctor's were baffled by my symptoms, so I was back and forth with them taking meds which made me tired and extra stressed out.

I finally started keeping track of his hours, something I had never done before, and began checking the cell phone bill. Hours and hours of calls appeared from a blocked number, some during his shift and others on his way to and from work. When I asked him about them, he said it was one of the guys from work. Then the calls came while he was home. When I would answer they would simply hang up.

He was becoming more distant and incredibly mean. This was not the man I had married.

One afternoon while the kids were at school, I decided to press the issue of why he wasn't getting paid for court and over time. I flat out asked him if he was having an affair. He vehemently denied it, and said that he had too much respect for me to do something like that. Even hearing those words, something didn't sit right within me. He had an excuse for everything. Finally I said I was going to call payroll and find out what the problem was with his checks. By this time the argument was extremely heated, and he finally confessed. He was having an affair with a dispatcher.

Shock does not even come close to what I was feeling. I thought I might pass out. The room was spinning and I felt as if I would vomit. I asked how long, when and where it started. He said it was over, and gave me a lame timeline, however, I wanted answers.

I couldn't function. I still did what I could do for the kids, but as for me. I was unable to eat because I couldn't keep food down. I ended up on blood pressure medicine due to my stress. I made him go get checked out by our doctor to make sure he didn't have any STDs. Fortunately our doctor was a Christian and let him know in no uncertain terms that what he was doing was wrong.

We decided we would stay together and work on things. But after a person has been hurt like that, trying to "fix" your marriage can almost seem like it is doing more harm than good. I wanted answers and he didn't want to give them to me. He continued to lie, and even if he did tell me the truth I couldn't believe him. The trust was gone.

Needless to say I didn't finish the *Love Dare*. As a matter of fact I believe I threw the book at him…literally. I couldn't concentrate enough. In the meantime I also got a job, thinking that would help. When he was angry he would make comments about me not working, so I reasoned that getting a job might help take some of the pressure off of him. I also increased my prayers. It became a full on conversation with Our Lord every minute of every day.

You see I wanted to save my marriage. I made a promise before God to stay with this man and I was not breaking any promises. I would lie next to him after he fell asleep and pray, "Please Lord, bring him home." I still felt very alone. I knew we needed help, but not just any help. I wanted someone who had the same beliefs about marriage and God that we did. I scoured the Internet looking for help. It was important that whomever we found was a Christian, and that they were somehow involved in Law Enforcement. It took me months to find the right one.

In the interim we were doing our best, but the Lord put on my heart that there was still something not right.

On a Sunday outing, we passed the exit to where the "destroyer" lived. When we got home, I checked the I-Pass and found all of the information I needed. My husband was still seeing her. When I confronted him with the proof, he lied and said the I-Pass was wrong. I wouldn't rest until it was all out in the open. Finally two days later he confessed....everything. Things I could not even imagine. She wasn't the only one; there were also several one-night stands.

I finally found the other woman's number. A friend of mine called it and gave her a piece of her mind. The woman told my friend that there were others, that she wasn't the only one my husband had been with, and then proceeded to call the police and file a report on me for harassment. I never even had a conversation with her.

This was now time to get serious. We found a couple who went through the same thing we did, and who were trained to deal with infidelity. They taught us that a marriage can't be healed as long as one is still involved with another person, nor can it be healed if Christ isn't the center of it.

For us, those truths were the beginning of the healing process. From that point on, we would take necessary steps to restore our marriage, such as regular date nights, having accountability partners to keep our marital eyes focused on one another, and finally, physically moving away from the past and embracing a new environment that was pleasing to both of us.

We were and are determined to make it work no matter what it takes.

In this police wife's marriage and so many like hers, stress mixed with an unbalanced foundation played into a whole host of other issues. Though she had a relationship with God, her husband did not, thereby leaving the marriage lopsided until it finally spun off into crisis mode. Then and only then, did the two get onto the same page. Today their marriage, though not without its bumps and battle scars, is stronger than ever, and they are spinning in one direction with God holding them together.

Lack of communication, infidelity, unmanaged anger, alcohol, drug usage, or other contributing factors can become a recipe for divorce. Good news? It *can* work and these statistics *can* become a thing of the past, but it's going to take both the husband and the wife to try and understand the other's mindset, then take steps to meet the challenges head on.

Let's now take a look at the biggest complaint in a law enforcement marriage.

The Communication Factor

I've heard it over and over *and* over. Communication or the lack there of, is the number one complaint in law enforcement marriages. Matter-of-fact in my own home, I've often answered myself just to keep the conversation going. Ha!

Think about the nature of our husband's job. From the time he clocks in on his shift, until he finally drags himself home, he's talking, responding, pushing paperwork, answering calls, making PR (public relations) appearances, etc. He's a counselor, a boss, a social worker, judge and jury, babysitter, coach, pastor, friend and employee. When he comes home, hopefully he's entering into his "safe zone." It is now okay to come off that high, try and relax, and mentally check out. I like to call it "defragmenting."

However, the short window of time they have driving from the station to the driveway is not long enough to process all the junk they've dealt with their entire shift. Though we as wives and significant others would like to believe they can just turn it off, it's really not that simple.

For the majority of our early marriage, I made the mistake of meeting Rick at the door with a barrage of questions, complaints, and much-needed adult conversation. It might have looked something like this:

> *Hey! I'm so glad you're home! Did you have a good day? I bet you're tired. I have dinner ready. You know, the school called today about (insert child's name here). They said he's failing his math class! You've got to talk to him. I can't believe it. I've done all I know to do. By the way, the neighbor came over complaining about (insert complaint). She just gets on my last nerve. I was wondering when you were going to be able to mow the lawn? It's really looking shabby.*

On and on, I would go without realizing that I was bombarding him with information overload. Instead of feeling as if he could come down off the high he'd been on all day, I was adding to it and now I might expect one of two responses. He would either:

1. Shut down and completely ignore what I was saying, or

2. Blow.

Since Rick tends to be more of a mellow fellow, the shut down response would commence, and I would feel isolated and left to wonder if I had done something wrong.

Let's look at the chart below:

# The Four Communication Skills

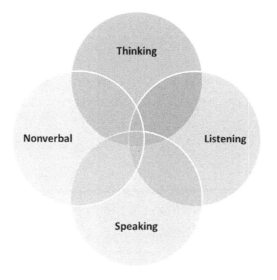

According to *Maximum Advantage: Psychology Applied to Life*, there are four basic skills in order to communicate effectively. (Communication Skills, 2008) Let's think of these in terms of a police officer.

On the job, an officer who is responding to a call needs to be *thinking* about the situation at hand, i.e. all the different scenarios, what could have happened, what might have actually happened, what the facts are, etc.

He needs to *listen* in order to hear what's being said or what's not being said.

He must be attuned to the *nonverbal* actions that are being displayed. Is there more to the story? Is the person or persons he's talking to fidgeting, looking away when talking, sweating, displaying closed-off body language through crossed arms, an obstinate look, seemingly ready to flee, etc.?

And finally, he needs to be able to effectively communicate or *speak back* in order to diminish the problem or offer a solution.

For a law enforcement officer, there is one more added circle:

Mental Alertness!

The officer *must* be mentally alert at all times in order to be aware of his surroundings and unseen threats to his personal safety or the safety of others.

With all of these senses heightened throughout the entire shift, the officer comes home and seemingly shuts down. With all responses slowed to a minimum output, and because he is now mentally, physically, and emotionally exhausted, oftentimes it results in continuous television surfing, gaming, scrolling of the phone, etc. These are the ways he defragments and even a simple question of "Where do you want to eat tonight?" can bring about the best "I don't care" answer or no response at all.

So what do you do? How can you help open the airways of conversation? I'll give you that in the next chapter. As for now, I want to challenge you to stop….give your officer time to get in the door, take a shower, change clothes and find a way to re-join the family unit before you or the children engage with him. I think you will begin to notice that even just this short window of time will make a world of difference in the type of communication you have afterword.

As for the officer, he must realize that reconnection to the family at some point is crucial to the health of the relationship. Wives and children need that quality time with their officer. It not only allows opportunity for communication, but helps to instill security and build bonds that are not easily broken. Both partners must be "all in" for this new direction to work. It takes time and effort, but is so worthwhile.

Remember this simple equation, "No connection = bad direction."

*"Reckless words pierce like a sword, but the tongue of the wise brings healing."* Proverbs 12:18

## Let's Talk

1. What was your experience with academy? How long? Were you married? Dating?
2. What do you think of the statistics Kristi shared? Do you agree? Disagree? Why?
3. Can you relate at all with Karen and Leroy's story? If so, how?
4. What is your opinion on the communication skills? Do you or your officer struggle with any of these skills and is there something you can do to "tune in" more effectively?

**Project:**

Try this exercise. You and your mate choose one or the other to be blindfolded. Next, stand the blindfolded person in the main room of your house, then direct him or her through verbal directions to safely find a certain item, such as a wallet, the television remote, or a piece of chocolate.

I know it sounds corny, but as you direct that person, hopefully both of you will see how important it is to have ongoing, clear communication. Without it, one or both of you would be terribly lost. Have fun!

## Chapter 4

*"Ultimately the bond of all companionship, whether in marriage or in friendship, is conversation."* – Oscar Wilde

As we discussed in the last chapter, communication is the number one complaint that I hear from both wives and officers. I think, though, before I give you a list of things you can do to help open the airways, I need to explain a little more about the difference between men and women and the way they take in information.

The Break Down

Several years ago, there was a book written by marriage experts Bill and Pam Farrel titled, *Men are Like Waffles, Women are Like Spaghetti.* Sounds intriguing, right? Ha! Actually this book, though it has a comical name, offers great insight into the minds of men and women. Let me see if I can break it down for you here:

| | = Waffles | Compartmentalizes - one box at a time |
|---|---|---|

| | = Spaghetti | Interconnects everything – one discussion leads directly into another, even if it doesn't have anything to do with the previous |
|---|---|---|

As described in the information above, men are like waffles. If you've ever looked at a waffle, you know it is one large square with a series of little squares within in it.

As a man takes in information, his brain processes that information one box at a time. That's not a bad thing by the way, just how God made them.

Women on the other hand can jump and loop around from one topic to the next just like a plate of spaghetti. We can go from talking about a friend's new baby in one sentence to complaining about the electric bill all in one breath! Quite an amazing feat, I assure you. Women understand each other's language; however, for the men in our life, it looks something like this:

> *Hey honey! I'm so glad you're home! Did*
> *you hear about Jan? She just had the baby.*
> *Had a girl, you know. I just knew she*
> *would. Looks so much like Dave. By the*
> *way, have you talked to Dave lately? We*
> *need to have them over. I think he's*

*working a lot of hours at the hospital,
though. Yeah, I heard that the hospital is
laying off a bunch of people. That's so sad.
I saw my friend Sara at the store and she
said that she may lose her job. You know
she's worked there for 20 years. She says
she may have to go back to school. By the
way, did you pick up the dry cleaning?*

Okay, so if you were to look deep inside the husband's brain, this is what you might see:

**Did you hear about Jan?...**

**?#$%??!!!\*&**

He hears the first sentence, then there's a hold placed on all other information until that first bit is processed. So what do we do? If you're like me, I automatically assume he's not listening and snap back with something like, "You are not listening to a thing I'm saying!"

In all actuality, he *is* listening, but is still trying to compartmentalize all the spaghetti you've given him. It's a process and as a woman, you or I can't expect our husband to jump around the boxes like we can.

Here's another example that I always use in my seminars. I think it effectively depicts the differences between men and women when it comes to a specific task.

## Mission: Go to Gap, Buy a Pair of Pants

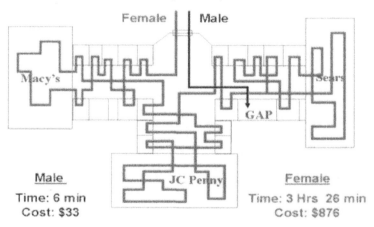

Now that you've had a good chuckle, you can see the mission is to go to the Gap and buy a pair of pants. The female goes in, weaves in and out, in and out, circles around and eventually reaches the Gap after three hours and twenty-six minutes, and at a cost of $876.

The male, however, goes in, makes a left buys the pants – six minutes and $33.

How true this diagram is in a funny kind of way. Men and women are different! We were designed that way and those differences help create a whole unit within the marital structure. However, when it comes to communication and the ways our specific nature processes and recognizes love within the relationship, those differences can cause difficulties if not understood by both the husband and the wife.

Defining the Situation

As we now know, men and women compute things in varying degrees. In our early years of marriage, I understood the fact that I had a need. That need was to reconnect to my husband after a period of separation, in order to feel loved and secure in the relationship. He on the other hand also had a need. He needed to be able to unwind, defragment and feel accepted and respected by me, not to mention sex, but that's another chapter. Wink.

Neither of us understood the other's need. If we had been given the information you are getting out of this book, then we may not have had to encounter some of the difficulties we did. Yet then again, we are both very hard headed and it may have taken something more like a kick in the leg in order to get our attention!

Let's now take a look at the situation between husband and wife upon re-entry:

Officer comes home after shift – Emotional shut-down

- Stressed

- Senses overload

- Physically, mentally, emotionally tired

- Energized through space and <u>respect</u>

- Living life one box at a time (Remember, he's a waffle!)


Wife comes home or has been at home – needs reconnection

- Is relational

- Gives her a sense of security

- Wants to be heard and feel important

- Is energized by attention and <u>love</u> from spouse (Definite spaghetti quality, here.)


So here's the breakdown. The officer comes home and, as we discussed, is sensory overloaded. Due to being on a high all shift long, he now emotionally and mentally shuts down upon re-entry into the home, looking for some down time to process all he's experienced. Remember, he's living one box at a time, and all his boxes are probably stacked on top of one another at this point.

In order for him to feel reconnected to his wife, he needs a bit of space and above all respect and acceptance for who he is as a man, provider, and husband.

She, on the other hand, is relational by nature. Women need to connect with other human beings in order to feel loved and secure, and especially with their spouse.

She wants to be heard and able to express her frustrations without the husband always having to "fix" it. This helps her feel as if she is important to him, and that what she does matters. She is energized by attention and outward expressions of love from her spouse.

And so it becomes a vicious cycle. If he's not receiving the respect he desires, he in turn will have a hard time showing her love. If he's not showing her love, she will have a hard time giving him respect. On and on it goes, where it stops nobody knows.

Things I Can Do to Help Communication and to Reconnect

With all of that said, there *are* things you can do to help ease the communication breakdown and reconnect with your spouse. The first and most important thing is to bend your knees. Say what? That's right. I'm surprised I don't have callouses on my knees from all the kneeling before the Lord in prayer, and not because I'm super spiritual, but because I was a desperate, crazy woman with a messed up marriage!

Remember the "glue" I mentioned in earlier chapters? That glue is God, and the only way to truly get the two of you on the same page, is if you spend time on your knees.

When he isn't talking….get on your knees.

When she is being irrational…get on your knees.

When the kids or in-laws are causing conflict within your home…get on your knees.

When everything is going perfectly…get on your knees.

I can't express to you the importance of a relationship with God, and the dire need for prayer within your marriage. It can move mountains that no other tip, trick or expert opinion can even come close to. 1 Thessalonians 5:16-18 says, *"Be joyful always; pray continually; give thanks in all circumstances, for this is God's will for you in Christ Jesus."* James 5:16b says, *"The prayer of a righteous man is powerful and effective."* That alone should give us the encouragement we need.

So, *do* you pray for your spouse…your kids…yourself? If not, I would encourage you to begin. Find a quiet place and get alone with God each day spending time to talk with Him as you would a good friend. Let Him know your frustrations and your fears. Ask Him to show you how to handle certain circumstances and give you wisdom. Thank Him for the ones He has placed in your life and for those moments when everything seems to be going well. He will hear you and He wants to have that relationship.

Second, encourage talk time. It sounds simple…maybe too simple. I'm sure you're thinking, but that's the whole issue. There isn't any.

Both of you *must* come to an agreement that there will always be a designated "talk time" within your relationship. This doesn't mean texting, emailing, or a quick phone conversation. I'm talking full on face-to-face conversation.

Husbands, put down the phone or gaming device. Wives, make sure those kiddos have something to do to keep them busy, then make the most of the time you have together. Pick a time when the two of you can sit down and effectively verbalize your frustrations, joys, concerns, excitements, etc. Your relationship MUST have face time or it is likely not to survive.

Third, be honest with one another. This does not mean that you belittle, accuse, nag or complain. The two of you need to agree to allow the other to communicate things that may be causing a rift within your relationship. For example:

> Wife: "Babe, I'm feeling as if you are spending more time at the station than you do at home. It really makes me feel unimportant." or

> Husband: "Honey, I'm having a hard time understanding your emotions."

As you can see, both the wife and the husband above are expressing actions or attitudes causing hurt feelings within the marriage. There's no screaming or yelling here, no accusatory tone, just plain honest expression of miscommunication issues.

Fourth, schedule that date night regularly and stick to it if at all possible! Lately, I have seen a number of wives posting pictures on social media of their first date night in over a year! If you gain nothing else from this book, realize this fact: Finding time away with your spouse from the mundane routine is crucial to the overall health of your marriage. It doesn't have to be expensive; a walk around the neighborhood or a movie and popcorn on the couch after the kids are in bed can qualify. Just make sure it is the two of you--alone--for more than ten minutes. I promise it will greatly reduce some of the tension you are feeling.

Fifth, get to know your spouse. Sounds simple enough. Before you married, I imagine you went to great lengths to find out what he or she liked to do, the music they enjoyed, movies they wanted see, etc. However, once we tie the knot, we somehow let down our guard and allow our spouse's interests to take a back seat to more pressing things such as bills, kids, work, etc.

Find ways to put excitement back into your marriage. Does he enjoy a certain sports team? Then secretly purchase tickets for the two of you to go on his day off. Does she have a particular hobby? Guys, I assure you, pottery class won't kill you. Go with her and brag on her accomplishments.

Finally, don't take things so personal. We all have a tendency to get our feathers ruffled when we feel as if we are being attacked, ignored or mistreated in some way.

Most of the time, when a wife snaps at her husband, or her husband shuts down, there's a deeper issue going on causing the immediate reaction. In essence, we are only seeing the symptoms of a bigger problem. So, don't take things so personal. Step back and analyze the situation. Perhaps she had a bad day at work or a stressful day with the kids. She's tired and needs a good night's rest. Is it possible that he had to deal with another child abuse case or notify another family that their loved one won't be coming home? Neither of these scenarios are license to mistreat or neglect your spouse, but they often *do* play a big part in ways we communicate.

She Says, He Says

> My husband and I have been married three months, and I feel as if our marriage is falling apart. My husband and I have both been under a lot of stress, but I still feel like I am not even a priority in his life. We've not been on any dates or had little if any time alone in the bedroom. I have expressed how I would like a few hours a week with him to go out and spend time together, but he has yet to take me up on it or even express interest. When he asks me what I want from him, I suggest all kinds of date

ideas, but he just shoots them down. I'm not sure what to do.

Here's a heart cry from a wife who is feeling left out and neglected. For whatever reason, her husband has absorbed himself in his work and has failed to recognize the needs of his spouse. Though there may be a simple explanation such as a new position taking up a lot of his time and attention, or possibly the stress of managing responsibilities of married life and work, or whatever it may be, it still boils down to his wife's needs are going unmet and the alarm bell is sounding.

Unfortunately, these warning bells go off continuously, unnoticed for weeks, months and even years until the one sending them gives up. We must train ourselves to tune in so we don't wake up one day to a note on the counter or a divorce paper in our mailbox. Here's another one:

> I have been an officer for 5 years. I know for me, the main issues have been time together. In the past I have expected my girlfriend to work around my schedule. Now I have to realize that she has a life outside of our relationship.
>
> **I know part of the problem on her end has been that I don't talk. I have a bad communication problem** and hate to argue. I deal with conflict at work and would rather

not have to deal with it at home. I don't trust people right off the bat like most do.

This officer realized his problem was with communication and spending quality time with his girlfriend. If we look closer at his last couple of statements, we see the typical shutdown response and "suspicious of everyone" behavior, evident in most law enforcement relationships.

I would venture to say that since he recognized these things, he and and his girlfriend have hopefully been able to work on their relationship. Yet, there are many who are still running around in their circles bumping up against each other instead of meshing together in one harmonious motion.

### Let's Talk

1. What do you think of the "waffle/spaghetti" theory?
2. Recognizing the differences in the way we communicate, are there steps you can take or are taking to make sure the message is clearly understood?
3. Do you currently or have you considered praying for your spouse daily? If you do pray, have you noticed a difference in his or her attitude toward you and the marriage?

4. Are you and your spouse able to have honest, face-to-face conversation? If not, why not?
5. Can you list important things about your spouse, such as his or her favorite food, favorite music, favorite hobby, favorite place to shop, or favorite book? If not, your homework assignment is to study your spouse and find out what makes them tick.

**Project:**

Take a few minutes to see how well you know your spouse. On a piece of paper for each, both number to 10, then answer the following questions about your spouse without their help. Finally, let them check over your answers. How'd you do?

1. What is your spouse's favorite color?
2. Favorite dessert?
3. Favorite place to visit?
4. Favorite song?
5. Favorite book/author?
6. Favorite breakfast food?
7. Favorite candy?
8. Favorite music group?
9. Favorite television show?
10. Favorite store?

# Chapter 5

*"Those who carried materials did their work with
one hand and held a weapon in the other."*
Nehemiah 4:17

## Manning the Walls

Back in biblical times, the great wall of Jerusalem
had been broken down and Nehemiah, the king's
cup-bearer had been granted leave from his duties to
go and repair it. The repairs, however, did not
come without conflict from outside forces. In order
to complete the task, the workers had to build the
wall with one hand and keep the other hand secure
on their weapon.

This story reminds me of the outside opposition we
can face as we try and protect our marriages.
Temptations, trials, poor choices, unforeseen
misfortune, and even friends and family, can create

chaos and destruction within even the most solid marriages. Therefore, we must be diligent as we build our relationships by doing all we can to help secure the boundaries, and keep tightly fastened to our spiritual weapon, which are prayer and God's written Word.

In the early years of our marriage, unfortunately, neither Rick nor I protected those boundaries as we should have. He was overwhelmed trying to balance work and home, and I was doing good just to keep my head above the fray, much less guard the doors. That's when jealousies began to enter and unhealthy relationships started to slip in.

Thankfully, God had other "soldiers" in place to pray and keep us accountable to God and to each other. After making a complete mess of our relationship, God moved us, not only physically, but spiritually as well. We ended up two hours north with not only a renewed sense of family and companionship, but also a deeper faith as we saw Him work things out on our behalf time and again. I guess you could say that was the beginning of our healing, though there would still be a few bumps in the road ahead.

Bob and Gina were struggling in their
marriage. Gina had asked Bob to move out
and give her space to think about the future
of their relationship. As a last resort, both
sought help from a good Christian counselor
and felt as if there might be some light at the
end of the tunnel, until Gina spent an entire
afternoon with a family member who had
total disdain for Bob. Gina was now
convinced that divorce was their only
option.

Ahh…family. We love them, but they can also be a
hindrance to our relationships. Part of manning the
walls is setting up boundaries for those closest to us.
Many of these folks are on a mission to invite us to
their misery. If they aren't happy, they don't want
anyone else to be. Word of warning here, be very
careful around these loved ones. Though we love
them and care about their opinions, it is easy to get
sucked into their vortex.

God commanded in Genesis 2:24, *"For this reason
a man will leave his father and mother and be
united to his wife, and they will become one flesh,"*
so, we must now place our loyalties with our
spouse. Though this does not give us license to be

ugly towards our family members, it does remind us that our responsibilities have now shifted. We are no longer under the supervision or direction of our parents, no longer a single unit journeying through this life, but now adults committed to a relationship ordained by God.

So what are some ways to "man" the walls, and what behaviors do we need to have in place in order to have a secure marriage?

First of all, every marriage needs a firm foundation. Rick and I have stumbled across a number of great people with a seemingly good marriage from the outside, but what we couldn't see was a cracked foundation underneath.

If you want a marriage to last through the stresses of time, heartache, disappointment, aggravation, worry, etc., then it's going to need Christ as the bedrock.

You may snarl at that or argue with me, touting stories of Christian couples who have divorced. The facts of the truth remains, two people who have learned to put God first in their marriage and in their own lives, and who make a conscious choice daily to walk in obedience to Him, find that their marriage will not only survive, but thrive.

An article written by Glenn T. Stanton in *The Christian Divorce Rate Myth*, states:

"Couples who regularly practice any combination of serious religious behaviors and attitudes -- attend church nearly every week, read their Bibles and spiritual materials regularly; pray privately and together; generally take their faith seriously, living not as perfect disciples, but serious disciples -- enjoy significantly lower divorce rates than mere church members, the general public and unbelievers." (Stanton G. T., Crosswalk.com, 2012)

Yes, there are Christian couples who have divorced. I've known many personally, and have grieved with them, but in each circumstance, at least one of them was not walking with the Lord. Show me a marriage that has failed, and I will show you a life or lives sidetracked with selfishness, pride, unforgiveness, resentment, or a whole host of other ungodly characteristics.

Secondly, a marriage that is going to withstand the pressures of the world must set boundaries. Think of boundaries as borderlines drawn to map out the "go" areas of your relationship, and the "stop" areas where we need to do an about face, and turn in the opposite direction.

For example, in our marriage, I know that after God, my husband comes first, and likewise it is God first, me second. If both of us have been working long hours and not had couple time, then no matter who comes knocking at the door or calling on the phone or messaging on social media, time with each other comes first. Everyone else will need to take a number and fall in line. It's not always easy, but is a conscious choice the two of us must make in order to reconnect with each other.

Likewise, if he has allowed things at work consume his time and has neglected to make our marriage a priority, or I've put the kids' needs/ministry needs before his, then there must be some re-evaluating and adjustments made.

We can get real good at allowing work, hobbies, kids, parents, friends, internet, or other things get in the way of our relationship. In and of themselves, each of these is not bad, but when they begin to take the place of time with our spouse or somehow undermine the marital covenant, then they become a parasite, which will eventually suck the life out of a marriage.

Boundaries also need to include interaction with others. In the world that we live in, it's nearly impossible to not come in contact with persons of the opposite sex. We work with them, we live next to them, we have them as friends, etc., but a solid marriage has learned to set up boundaries or accountability lines around those relationships.

For many law enforcement marriages, infidelity has become a huge issue. With long hours put in at the station coupled with the exclusiveness of the job and lack of quality time with their spouse, many officers have let their guard down and become emotionally attached to a co-worker or other person of interest, leading to physical intimacy outside the boundary of marriage. And, it's not just officers. Many spouses have succumbed to their loneliness and resentment over the absence of their officer husband or wife, and have simply looked elsewhere to find connection. We definitely must safeguard our marital walls.

Tammy had a great job and was climbing the corporate ladder. With exotic trips and a pretty hefty salary, she felt as if John's ultimatum between her job and divorce was irrational and on the verge of abusive. John was a full-time officer and having a hard time balancing his job, care of the children, and the strain her absence put on their relationship. Who was in the wrong?

Situations such as the above scenario can wreak havoc on a marriage, and if the couple is not seeking out God's direction and the best interest of their spouse and family, more-often-than-naught those types of relationships will end in divorce.

Tammy can represent many women and men who choose career over marriage. The prestige of a high paying job with all its perks can definitely be a deal breaker when it comes to marital harmony, yet scriptures tell us "the love of money is a root of all kinds of evil," and that some people "have wandered from the faith and pierced themselves with many griefs" because of it.

So how do we combat things like this? Though ultimately it is a heart issue, there are some things to remember. Such as:

1. Wall building (Marriage) takes work and time. Stay at it!

2. Always put your spouse's needs, thoughts, desires, above your own…it is no longer "me" but "we".

3. No job, hobby, sport or handbag is worth more than the spouse God has given you. Treasure your relationship, for it is more precious than gold.

4. Realize that you can't fix your spouse, you can only fix you.

5. Whatever you put into your marriage is exactly what you will get out of it.

6. Agree from the start that divorce will NOT be an option. Don't even let it be brought to the table.

7. Physical intimacy in marriage is vital, but don't expect it if you are not displaying love outside of the bedroom.

8. Get unrealistic ideas out of your head. There's no such thing as a perfect marriage, because there are no perfect people.

9. Never stop dating.

10. Always have your spouse's back. Always.

## Let's Talk

1. Do you believe specific boundaries in marriage are a good idea? Why or why not?
2. Have you ever had to deal with a family situation that caused strain in your relationship?
3. What are some ways that help you keep your marriage "in check"?

4. What are some boundaries that both you and your spouse need to work on?

**Project:**

Take a moment to write down some thoughts to your spouse. Some examples of content may be:

➢ Describe what it was that drew you to him or her? Was it her eyes, his smile, or the way he laughed?
➢ Describe the moment you realized your husband/wife was "the one".
➢ What are five things you love about your husband/wife?

Have fun with it! Be sure to share your thoughts with your spouse only.

## Chapter 6

*"As my husband climbs the ladder at work, he is less available (physically and emotionally) at home. I'm having a hard time adjusting to life without his involvement. I have health issues, a child with ADHD, and a toddler who's into everything. Needing some prayers today!"*

Parasites and Wall Mites

We all face threats to our marriage. They may be as huge as infidelity or as small, if we can call it that, as resentment. Whatever they are, these parasites and wall mites can get into the very fabric of our marital relationship and do long lasting damage.

Over the next several pages, I want to cover a myriad of these pesky varmints and explore more about what makes each tick, as well as ways to safeguard our wall from attack. But first, let me tell you about Diane and Andre.

Diane was a fun-loving, outgoing young woman who loved to socialize and be constantly on the go. When she married Andre, he was not yet an officer, and wanted to do whatever it took to please Diane. Upon finishing academy, Andre quickly became bogged down in work and the stresses of the job, no longer desiring to go out with Diane and her friends, but rather sit at home and relax on the couch. Quickly the marriage began to erode. Diane felt stifled in the marriage feeling as if she was no longer an important part of Andre's life. To her, it seemed, he was much more interested in himself and his needs, than her and her needs. Andre viewed it as selfishness on her part, not understanding that he was physically, mentally and emotionally drained. After a year or so of fighting and bickering, the marriage ended and Diane and Andre went their separate ways.

As we've discussed previously, two of our biggest threats to our marital walls are a lack of communication and time with our spouse. Both husband and wife *must* make a conjoined effort to keep these two things a priority. With that said however, let's explore additional parasites that can cause a lot of heartache.

Alcoholism

Visit any FOP lodge or cop hangout, and you are bound to find alcohol and lots of it. It's no secret that most cops look for ways to de-stress from all the junk they daily experience, and alcohol is often the tool they use.

Milwaukee Chief, Ed Flynn was once quoted as saying, *"We're all aware that alcohol abuse is a problem of the job. For as long as there have been police officers, alcohol has been a problem in policing. Cops use alcohol for a variety of reasons. They use it to de-stress, they use it to relax with each other. This is all a problem, of course, because alcohol affects conduct. We have a lot of officers who are arrested for DWI, and a lot of officers involved in other alcohol-related problems off duty. And we had three suicides my first year in this department, all of whom were under the influence when they killed themselves."* (Police Chiefs Discuss a Tough Issue: Alcohol and Drug Abuse by Officers, 2012)

Large amounts of alcohol consumption by anyone can and will pose significant problems, but especially within an LE marriage. Let's take for example the following well-known side-effects:

- It impairs judgment

- It alters emotions, behaviors, and moods

- It slows your response time

- Suicide rate heightens to 5-10 more than line-of-duty-deaths

- May cause loss of job which in turn might contribute to loss of family

Think about it this way. If stressed out Officer Bob comes home after spending a couple of hours at the lodge drinking a number of beers, he is potentially more likely to:

- Get in an argument with his wife
- Yell at the kids for insignificant matters
- Crash on the couch or the Lazy Boy, further shutting down all communication
- Negate his responsibilities as a husband/father/man of the home, etc.

The other issue is that a number of officers find themselves in trouble with the same law in which they swore to honor, serve and protect.

Several years ago, I was invited to speak at a law enforcement function out-of-state, along with a number of others. One of the speakers was an attorney for a large FOP organization. After presenting insight on a number of legal situations involving officers, he began to joke about the number of cops he represents for DUIs. Hmm.

Then there is this example, a former Connecticut officer arrested three times in eleven hours for DWI and shoplifting charges. I would venture to say that not only did he lose his job, incur jail time, and tarnish his reputation for life, but if he was a married man, I would have to assume there were serious repercussions at home as well. (Former Connecticut police officer arrested 3 times in 11 hours on drunken-driving charges, 2014)

Another tragic by-product of alcohol is cop suicide. Dr. Kevin Jablonski, Chief Psychologist for LAPD noted that, "Almost every officer who commits suicide was under the influence of alcohol at the time and had a history of alcoholism." (Police Chiefs Discuss a Tough Issue..., 2012)

Coupling alcohol to the stresses of the job then adding in frustrations and problems within the marital unit can often spell out a recipe for self-destruction. I'm not saying that all officers who drink and have marital problems will commit suicide, but what I am saying is that they often go hand-in-hand.

Though a casual drink at a social function is usually not a cause for alarm, when alcohol becomes a crutch for those who need help in just coping to get by, then there is a greater problem that needs to be addressed

With all that said, let's not solely pick on the officer. Many wives are having some of the very same issues. In order to deaden the pain of loneliness, exhaustion, anxiety, and stresses, these women are drinking themselves silly, only to find that eventually the intoxication wears off and the problems still exist.

In our marriages, we *must* be vigilant to hold each other accountable when it comes to alcohol and the obsessive consumption of this mind-altering drug. It can and will destroy you and your marriage if not kept under control and within appropriate boundaries.

Drug Usage – Prescription or Otherwise

As we all are aware, being a law enforcement officer is not easy, and because of the nature of their job, many find themselves using coping mechanisms such as alcohol or drug usage to deal with the everyday crud.

Oftentimes an addiction might begin with a work-related injury requiring pain medication to ease the burden, or to help cope with psychological issues such as bouts of anxiety, depression or sleeplessness resulting from a traumatic event or series of events.

Doctors may prescribe a painkiller such as Oxycontin or Oxycodone, or a steroid of some sort, and a cycle of dependency begins as levels of relief increase with dosages over time.

However, there are also the even darker instances. Those officers working undercover assignments who are being exposed and falling prey to the seedy underworld of hard-core street drugs and criminal activity.

Take for example former Greater Manchester Undercover Officer Rob Carroll, who fell into heroin addiction and was jailed for giving police-issued weapons to his dealer. Carroll is quoted as saying,

> "I was hallucinating. I got to the point where I was more comfortable being my alter ego Lee Taylor than I was being me. It was when I was Rob Carroll that I was acting the father, the family man and husband. That's how bad I got. When you are a smackhead you are so ashamed, it's the worst thing you can possibly be." (Corcoran, 2014)

In 2012, Sean Riley, former officer and recovering drug addict cited that multiple studies suggest drug addiction amongst law enforcement was in upwards of 20-25%. (Riley, 2012)

So what gives? What happens when an officer falls into a cycle of drug addiction, lies and cover ups? His or her marriage (if there is one), tends to completely unravel as well as his or her career and life overall. Once the seed has been sewn, it is a hard, long journey to overcome it, but it *can* be done with the right help, attitude and support, especially if that officer and his spouse have a firm foundation rooted in God.

We are reassured with these words from Isaiah 43:2, *"When you go through deep waters, I will be with you. When you go through rivers of difficulty, you will not drown. When you walk through the fire of oppression, you will not be burned up; the flames will not consume you."* NLT

God is our strength during those times of struggle. Only *He* can bring us through to a place of true healing.

Violence and Abuse

When I began to do my research on problems within an LE family, I had never even factored in the statistics on domestic violence situations. Yet it is there and a very real problem that certainly takes a toll on marriages and homes across the country.

- According to Purple Berets, in a nationwide survey of 123 police departments, 45% had no specific policy for dealing with officer-involved domestic violence. In that same survey, the most common discipline imposed for a sustained allegation of domestic violence was counseling.

- Domestic Violence is Law Enforcement's Dirty little secret. Only 19% of departments indicated that officers would be terminated after a second sustained allegation of domestic violence.

- In San Diego, a national model in domestic violence prosecution, the City Attorney typically prosecutes 92% of referred domestic violence cases, but only 42% of cases where the batterer is a cop. (Domestic Violence in Police Families, 2003)

What's happening within many of our departments is that crimes such as this are being swept under the rug instead of being reported and dealt with. These things are messy and give the badge as a whole a black eye.

Officers are called to be men and women of integrity and truth, not committing some of the same crimes of those they are arresting. Yet as we all know, our officers are also human. They get angry, they hurt, they bleed and they die the same as everyone else. Does that make it right for them to abuse their spouse, or drink their way into oblivion? Certainly not, but it does reveal a deeper truth –

they need hope; something or *Someone* who can change their entire mindset.

The problems these officers are facing are nothing new. The root of each of these issues has been around since time began. It is called sin, and that sinful behavior can cause even the most prominent, well-versed, highly educated, even religious person to crash and burn into a pit of despair and harmful cycle of abuse, addiction or other painful choices.

Take for instance the tragic incident in Spanish Fork, Utah, in January of 2014. Lindon Police Officer Joshua Boren used his service weapon to execute his wife, their two children and his mother-in-law, after his wife had accused him of being drugged and raped against her will on several different occasions.

Spanish Fork Lt. Matthew Johnson said the couple had been experiencing marital problems in the past few months, but that Joshua had appeared upbeat and displayed no signs of depression before the killings. Johnson was quoted as saying that there "were no warning signs." (Joshua Boren, Police Officer in Spanish Fork, UT, Kills 4 Family Members Then Himself, 2014)

I beg to differ with Lt. Johnson's assessment. There were clear warning signs when he began to have marital problems. Again, I'm not implying that every officer with an unstable home life is going to take out his family, but what I *am* saying is that he was in a stressful job with a boiling pot at home. That mixture could lead to violence, and a great majority of the time lead to divorce.

What if this officer and his wife had received some type of peer support? What if someone had recognized his need for assistance? Could it have been prevented? Would it have made a difference? Could five lives still be in tact? No one really knows for certain, but I believe this officer felt as if he was out of options. Hope had run out and this was his last resort.

In order to stop the cycle of abuse, we must speak up and recognize when an officer is in distress. A home front under fire is a sure sign that there could be further trouble ahead.

Another case of domestic violence and marital strife gone too far, is the recent murder/suicide of recently retired White Plains, New York officer Glen Hochman, who after having ongoing discussions with his wife about divorce, shot and killed his two teenage daughters, his three dogs and himself in their home. The wife and their eldest daughter were not home at the time. (Fitzgerald, 2015)

What a tragedy to believe that a man who just last May received the department's life-saving award for keeping an unresponsive man alive until paramedics could get on scene, could take the lives of those he loved the most, not to mention his own life.

How could this situation have been avoided? Were there warning signs? What if someone had tried to help the couple reconcile? Would that have stopped the violence? No-one is certain, but what we do know is that there are many more out there suffering at the hands of an abuser who just happens to be a cop.

Isolation

As far as isolation, that tendency is nothing new either. It seems that this "us" against "them" mentality has been around as long as there has been law enforcement. However, it can grow to an unhealthy level as the officer pulls himself/herself farther and farther away from society, friends and family.

Within the marital unit, if the officer isolates himself, he is also isolating the family. Friends the couple once hung out with are now a distant memory. No longer does he want to go out and do anything in a social setting, and the wife is left feeling lonely and empty.

If a marriage is going to thrive, a law enforcement couple is going to have to rise above the tendency to isolate. Finding and establishing friendships outside of the law enforcement world is a necessity and will help to keep a healthy balance between the relationship and the badge.

PTSD (Post Traumatic Stress Disorder)

Did you know that every 17 hours a law enforcement officer commits suicide? Many of these deaths can directly be linked back to a form of PTSD. (Dr. Jean G. Larned, 2010)

Thankfully, many choose to remain and fight the fight, however, they simply do not seek professional help or even realize that with the right type of treatment, their symptoms can be alleviated. That is where organizations such as Serve & Protect, a non-profit serving all first responders and their families through 24/7/365 crisis line, chaplain alliance, and therapist alliance, come into play.

Robert Michaels, Founder of Serve & Protect says, "We wrestle through the wants, needs, desires, and yes, the pain that can overwhelm our Heroes. Even Heroes want to be safe, to be respected, and to be appreciated. Together we unpack the issues. Sometimes it's the trauma of the job or the stress of daily living. It may be finances, marriage failure or addictions. It is anything that makes life unmanageable. We do this in absolute confidentiality, and we see it through to help our Heroes reclaim healthy lives." (Michaels)

Symptoms of this parasite can display itself at anytime and in anyone who has faced a traumatic event.

Not all law enforcement personnel will experience PTSD, but it's no secret that all law enforcement/first responder will encounter trauma. Whether it is a horrific accident, homicide scene, house fire with casualties, shooting, etc., memories and pint up emotions from those events can display themselves even years down the road.

The officer may experience hypervigilance, anger/rage, sleep disorders, anxiety and depression, relationship issues, emotional disconnect, social withdrawal, suicidal thoughts, aggressive alcohol consumption, and/or anger with God.

The officer may become hardened or calloused, filled with cynicism, suspicion and distrust. Families, especially spouses having to deal with these issues often feel helpless in knowing what to say or how to cope.

If left unchecked, PTSD can destroy a marriage, a family and the person who is experiencing it first-hand.

A number of years ago, a seasoned officer experienced a horrific scene while on patrol. He was first to answer the call to a family murder/suicide. His thoughts kept replaying the scene of holding the toddler in his arms as she struggled to take her last breaths. Though he tried to stuff it down and continue on with life as normal, it finally cost him his whole career. This officer was unable to cope with the recurring nightmares and scenes playing out in his head. As a way to try and shut out the pain, he shut himself off from most everyone, including close friends and previous co-workers. Thankfully, his marriage has stayed intact.

Situations such as the one just described can cause lasting effects on an officer. Rick and I have not only witnessed it in so many we minister to, but have also experienced a taste of it firsthand in our own marriage.

Several years ago, after working a series of fatal accidents coupled with a frightening episode of a physical struggle he and another officer had with a woman holding a gun to her chest, Rick quickly grew silent. He began to lose interest in everyday things. I felt him slipping away into some type of dark abyss.

Work and home life became overwhelming for him. He struggled to maintain that sense of normalcy and eventually took a full-time job at a furniture warehouse to give himself a break, but making sure to keep enough hours at the PD to ensure that his POST not expire.

For an entire year he wrestled with his thoughts, and slowly I could see an improvement in the way he related to the kids and me. After much prayer and patience on my part (lessons I had to learn), I sensed him returning to the marriage and to his calling.

After a year, Rick was ready to return to full-time duty. Though I'm guessing the thoughts of those horrific events still haunted him for some time, his faith in God grew stronger and ultimately became his lifeline in finding true inner peace, not to mention our marriage became rock solid.

Here is where I want to end this chapter. After all that negativity, I feel it important to again reiterate...you *can* get through it. Though some, if not all of these situations seem hopeless, with God, anything is possible.

Stay the course!

*"Even when I walk through the darkest valley, I will not be afraid, for you are close beside me. Your rod and your staff protect and comfort me."* Psalm 23:4 NLT

Let's Talk

1. In your marriage, have either of you struggled with any one of the above mentioned parasites? If so, how did you overcome/cope?
2. What steps might you as a couple take to protect the boundaries of your marriage from situations such as these?
3. How important do you think communication within the marriage is in dealing with the above?

**Project:**

Find a way to show encouragement and support to the officers and spouses in your spouse's department.

Suggestions might include:

- Host a LE Marriage Seminar (wink)
- Plan an appreciation day for law enforcement families
- Take snacks/goodies to the department and pass them out (For large precincts, you may only be able to cover one shift or squad....that's okay!)
- Talk to your church or community center to see if you could host a movie night for

families using their facility. Provide a kid-friendly movie, popcorn (sometimes movie theaters will donate), etc. for LE families to enjoy

Have fun with it and know that you are spreading some encouragement!

# Chapter 7

*"Happy are those who dare courageously to defend what they love."* - Ovid

Protecting Your Marriage Sexually

The Affair

I remember back to the first time I heard about a police officer having an affair with a dispatcher in the same department--Rick's department. It threw up a whole host of fears inside me as I put myself in the place of the wife. *How could So-in-So do that to his family? How could the other woman live with her choice to break up a marriage? Would it happen to us?*

Yet, working out in public for many, many years, I have seen it first hand over and over. It doesn't just affect police officers, nor does it only happen to certain types of people. Anyone can fall prey to this parasite that so easily entangles many folks and wrecks countless relationships and lives. And, it often begins when one party is feeling disconnected to his or her spouse/significant other.

Let's look at some ways we can become disconnected from our spouse:

1. **Lack of communication** – We've pretty much already covered this, but communication is key to a healthy relationship. Couples must have time to reconnect verbally in order to keep the bond intact.

2. **Lack of courtship** – It may seem old fashioned, but I believe our grandmas and grandpas had it right. Courtship should not end once we get married. People change over the years...their interests, likes, dislikes, and it is our job to continually figure out what makes our spouse tick. It is vital that we find those things that please our spouse and do them. Even little things like flowers, love notes, loading the dishwasher or filling up the car can go a long way to woo our mate.

3. **Lack of commitment** – Many folks in today's society simply do not have the tenacity to commit to something as binding as marriage. It is perfectly acceptable to just live with the one we love, instead of committing to that person for life through a

marital relationship. Though it may be viewed as convenient or no big deal, it displays a lack of an "all-in" mentality. How many car dealerships would allow you to drive a brand new car off the lot and use it for the next ten years without ever signing on the dotted line? Probably not any. They want you to commit to purchasing the car and making it your own ever before you can actually take it off the lot. Likewise, commitment to staying in the game even when it gets tough is also lacking. Many simply give up the fight because they don't "feel" love anymore or don't have the umph to make it work. It all boils down to self and whether we have our focus on self or on the needs of our spouse/significant other.

4. **Lack of sex** – I remember being a young mom with three little ones, a full-time job, a messy house and no energy for sex. Frankly, at times the thought detested me. However once I realized how important sex was to the health of my marriage and how it actually could be a stress reliever, I was more apt to being willing in the bedroom. Girls, sex is one of THE most important aspects of marriage for your husband. He needs it physically. He needs it psychologically. He needs it to reconnect with you. He needs it often! I know there's a lot more to it than what I can give in this

little paragraph, but hear me when I say, you won't regret it. Guys...your wife needs to know she is the most important thing in your life ALL the time, not just in bed. Show her love, gentleness and attention in everyday moments, and I'll guarantee you will have a woman who will be more responsive to you when you most want her.

5. **Lack of God** – Here she goes again, that God talk. Yes, because Rick and I have learned the hard way. When we didn't have God first and foremost in our lives, our marriage began to crumble, even in the area of attractions to others. Thankfully, God intervened and physically moved us away from what could have been a potential threat physically to our marriage. After we realized that God was what we both were lacking, all other physical/mental aspects of the relationship (fighting, jealousies, prideful tendencies, selfish gratification, etc.) became more manageable. God was the key to our success and still is.

Let's take into account some other facts in regards to sexual parasites and the way they can affect our relationships:

- Fact: Men are stimulated visually

- Fact: Officers/first responders are continually bombarded with stimuli which are sexual in nature (magazines, porn, pictures, naked people, etc.)
- Fact: Both men *and* women have opportunity to come in frequent contact with people of the opposite sex through work, social events, etc.
- Fact: Certain movies/books/websites are becoming a hot ticket item (literotica) for women, leaving lasting thoughts and impressions that usually do not correlate with real life.
- Fact: Pornography is easily accessible and both men *and* women are being drawn into this delusional obsession.

Couple all these things with an unhappy marriage/marital partner, and it often opens up to things such as an affair.

Again, I just want to stress to you the importance of marriage and how worth it is to fight for it. Having your best friend to wake up to every day doesn't happen overnight. It takes time, patience and perseverance on both parts. It takes commitment and a lot of love. Finally, it takes limitless prayer, but in the end, you'll be blessed to have a marriage that has withstood the test of time.

Pornography

I felt it important to address this subject as well. Many marriages and relationships have been affected by pornography and its addictive attraction.

Just recently, I ran across a blog written by a housewife and mom to a couple of toddlers. She admitted that late at night after the kids were in bed and the stresses of the day were coming to a close, she chose to unwind by feasting on a delectable diet of pornography. She at first tried to justify it by thinking she was helping her marriage. *Wouldn't her husband be turned on to her if she was already visually stimulated?*

However, over time, the toll it took on her marriage and attitude toward sex with her husband was clearly evident. She no longer felt satisfied by the predictable love-making she was accustomed to, and the focus of her unhappiness was all focused on self and her own gratification.

Pornography not only destroys relationships, but it also destroys lives. For law enforcement officers, they know the behind scenes effects of the porn industry and how it preys upon young women, teenagers and children, using their vulnerabilities to satisfy the appetites of those obsessed with self.

In a web of crime, money schemes, and lewd, indecent conduct, many people have been scarred for life by the exploits of these sites. For that reason alone, we should run from them instead of getting sucked into this type of parasitic activity.

Earlier this year, Rick and I had the privilege of speaking at a first responder marriage seminar in Florida. While we were there, we were given a tour of one of the Sheriff's departments in the area in which we spoke.

I remember walking down the long hallway to where the detectives working the sex crime unit were stationed. Two of them were in a room that was dark and full of electronic equipment. Another two or three of them were in a separate room with huge monitors set up for continuous viewing of images of children, women, etc. being raped, assaulted, or otherwise preyed upon.

My heart wept for them as I thought about the mental damage this must do to their psyche day in and day out. Matter-of-fact, the officer who was giving us the tour described how many of these detectives display a form of PTSD from all the junk they continuously digest.

Pornography and any form of online or written sexually explicit material will have a negative effect on you, your thoughts and your marriage whether you believe it or not. Sex was created to be shared in love between husband and wife to establish the bonds of oneness as well as procreation, yet what much of it has become is wholly against God and against what is healthy and natural for each of us.

For those of you who must view this stuff for the sake of your job and of others, I pray for you and ask God to cover and protect your thought life. It takes a special breed of people to be able to process all the junk and still maintain a "normal" life.

As we wind up this chapter, I want to stress this point to you--sex is God created and should only be shared with the one you have chosen to be your husband or wife. Protect yourself and your home from this parasite worming its way into your life and marriage. Avoid situations if at all possible where you and another person of the opposite sex are together alone. Discuss personal things with your spouse only. Be cautious of physical contact with others who are not your spouse.

Whatever it takes to guard the wall...guard it. If your computer is a stumbling block, then throw it out. Better to be computer-less than to get sucked into something that will destroy your marriage.

If your television is a problem, get rid of it. Your marriage will actually be stronger if you're not lured in to all that mindless trash and can spend time together.

I know you can do this!  With God all things are possible.

Let's Talk

1. How important do you think it is to protect the walls of your marriage from the above sexual parasites?
2. Do you agree or disagree with Kristi's take on the importance of marriage and the reasons behind her passion for protection?
3. Have you or someone you know ever been in a situation where the walls were not well protected? How did you or the person handle the situation?

**Project:**

Have a date night with your spouse that will leave him or her wanting more!  Plan out an intimate dinner for two or a sexy scavenger hunt throughout your town or home that offers clues for what is awaiting at the end. Enjoy each other...this is the fun part of marriage! ♥

If you like, journal your experience here:

# Chapter 8

*"Father's Day logistics...Husband is on afternoons. He has to leave tomorrow by 2:30 PM to make it to the station. Problem is when he gets home tonight at 3:00 AM he will sleep until 11:30 AM, and I will not be home from church until 2:45. Do I leave the cards on the table for when he wakes up? Wake him up at 7:30 AM for a few minutes for the kids to say hi? Or just wait until Monday? Crazy life!"*

Kids and stress

I never gave it a second thought as our children were growing up. I banked on them unfortunately having insecurities from the years Rick and I did not get along, rather than the law enforcement career itself. However, it wasn't until I wrote my book *Standing Courageous*, that I realized just how much the job affected them.

In the book, our daughter submitted her thoughts on how she worried about her dad and that every day at 7:18 (her dad's badge number) she would say a prayer for him and all the other officers in his department. Had I known at the time these things were swirling through her head, I would have made sure we gave her the reassurance and coping mechanisms to help in times of fear.

One thing to remember, is though kids are more in tune with things than we give them credit, they are also resilient, which is a blessing in how they cope with this not-so-normal life.

Let's take a look at a partial list of some sources of stress put out by *The Police Chief* online magazine:

- Shift work and overtime – missed events and occasions

- Excessively high expectations of their children

- Avoidance, teasing, or harassment of the officer's children by other children because of the parent's job

- Presence of a gun in the home

- Officer's 24-hour-a-day role as a law enforcer

- Perception that the officer prefers to spend time with coworkers rather than with his or her family

- Family members' perception of the officer as paranoid or excessively vigilant and overprotective of them

➢ Critical incidents, or the officer's injury or death on the job (Sam Torres, 2015)

Looking through the list, I would have to say that the officer's on-going absence is probably the most frustrating to kids. When dad or mom has to miss a special school play or crucial ballgame, it's hard for them to understand that it's part of the job and not necessarily the parent's desire.

Also, officers tend to be a little tougher on their own kids when they've dealt with thugs on the street all day. I remember many arguments ensuing over our oldest son and the way his dad wanted to "make" him do this or that. It is hard for an officer to see his or her son or daughter as a unique individual and not as a potential train wreck if he or she isn't doing well in school, talking to less-than-desirable other kids, quitting band, etc.

I'm definitely *not* saying that children shouldn't be held to a higher standard and have expectations placed on them, however, I think sometimes we can try and mold them into a box that doesn't align up with their own unique abilities and gifts. If they quit band against your wishes, perhaps we need to open our eyes and see they are just not musically inclined, but rather are artsy or sports minded. Cut some slack. Loosen up. Often times it is just them trying to spread their wings, yet don't let them get by with disrespect or ungodly behaviors. That is a whole different story.

Another issue that arises in an LE household is when a child wants to go to a sleepover at Jimmy's house or a sweet 16 party at Paige's. These are the moments that you have to put on your mean-guy parenting hat and try and explain without divulging information as to why your child cannot go to these children's homes. I've had to use excuses like...

*Daddy has been to his house before and it just wouldn't be a good situation.*

*There are just some things happening there that aren't appropriate. Why don't you ask Paige to come to your house on another day?*

Of course, I've had the slammed doors, the pouts and the roll of the eyes, but we made it and you will too. It's just part of our LE life unfortunately.

As far as a gun in the home, I'm not sure children really stress over one being in the home, but I do know a family whose little four year old boy got a hold of dad's service gun and shot and killed himself. That is just something a person never recovers from. So moms and dads, please make sure those things are put up and away from the little ones and even curious teenagers. I'd hate to see another family go through something so tragic.

Finally there is the fear of dad or mom getting shot and not coming home. Kids definitely pick up on these things. Especially being in a law enforcement family, officer shootings or deaths are often talked about within the home or viewed through posts on social media sites, etc.

Just as our daughter worried about her dad, children are not immune to feelings of fear or anxiety over "the bad guys" out to do harm to our loved one.

In an article I read, one officer described a time when he and his wife were signing a contract stating he would always wear his vest. Upon laying the paper on the table and leaving the room, the officer's three sons all signed their little names under their momma's signature.

These children were in essence stating that their dad's safety was of upmost importance and they wanted to make sure he returned home to them after the end of his shift. Priceless.

So what are some ways we can help our children cope with the stresses of the job? Below are a few ideas that might help them feel a little more in control and a little less stressed.

- Encourage children to ask questions about mom or dad's job

- Talk on their level – not too much, not too vague

- Focus on the positives

- Allow them to give input in family decisions

- Let them plan "outings" or special activities for the whole family

- "Date" each child – find time when dad or mom can take the child out for special one-on-one time

- Pray with them and for them

Again, kids are resilient. Though from time to time they may wrestle with feelings of anxiety, allowing them to have a small part in the overall family structure helps to empower them and equip for those difficult times.

Officers should talk with their children about their job, not giving too much information, but enough to satisfy their curiosity. A trip to the station getting to know the other officers on his or her shift or squad can also help them feel more comfortable.

Be sure and focus on the positives. Think of good things that happened – someone you helped, a good deed you did, a card of thanks you received, etc. that helps them know that there is a positive side as well.

Dating each child is also important. Rick was always so good about picking a special day for each of the kids when he would take just that one to breakfast before school or stop by and eat lunch with the other. Special occasions for our daughter such as birthdays were also recognized with flowers in the school office with a note that said *I love you*.

For dads especially, these moments mean so much to your children. You will probably never know how much that extra show of love and attention will mold your child's heart and character.

Finally, pray with your children. Whether or not you are "religious," prayers for and with your kids go a long way in not only letting them know you care for their physical and spiritual well-being, but also it empowers them with God's help to overcome obstacles in their life, fears, frustrations, and points them to the One who can give them wisdom to make wise decisions as they grow. Extremely crucial!

My husband works nights in a bad area. Lately our boys have been really noticing that dad misses out, especially the four year old. Today he got home after working a 15 hour shift and was totally drained. The boys were super excited to see him, so he told them to let him sleep for four hours then wake him up at 3:00 and he will take them outside to play! When it was time to wake up daddy, our son (being all boy), goes up to our room and yells at my husband who instantly screams at him to stop because he's sleeping. When he finally does get out of bed, he has a short temper and yells at both of them for being too loud. Ten minutes later I approach him and apologize. He stops me by saying "Until you stop talking down to me you can (explicative)". I instantly began to cry and told him he cannot talk to me like that and asked him to leave, but he refused. Not a good day!

Our little ones *and* big ones want so much to spend time with dad or mom on his or her day off. The way we handle the times we are tired or stressed can and will affect how they handle their own stresses. Be mindful of them and try to recognize their needs as well as your own. Remember, these are the people who really matter. Let them know often how much you love and care for them.

## Let's Talk

1. Has your child(ren) ever displayed any type of anxiety or fear over his or her parent's occupation?
2. What are some things your family has done to help the kids feel secure and a part of the overall family dynamics?

3. How do you as a parent help yourself deal with the tiredness and stress, so in turn you can help your kids?


## Project

Plan an outing for the whole family such as bike riding, a picnic, basketball in the park or just a fun evening at home with games and a family-friendly movie. A parent doesn't have to spend big money on fancy toys, for what these little ones really want is time. Have fun!

## Chapter 9

*"If you live to be a hundred, I want to live to be a hundred minus one day, so I never have to live without you."* – Winnie the Pooh


It Can Be Done!

As we've covered most everything a law enforcement/first responder marriage may go through, I just want to encourage you that though it is tough, it can be done. Let me finish the rest of our story for you as testament to this truth.

In 1996, our marriage wasn't horrible, but it wouldn't have won the greatest marriage award, either. We had three little ones all under the age of 6. I was working full-time at our county courthouse and Rick was still going ninety to nothing in law enforcement, though his department had gone downhill over the years leading up to this time. Rampant moral corruption and politics made life pretty miserable for him. It had come down to basically a "just keep your nose clean and your head above water" job, but he wanted out. We were just not sure how or if that would happen.

Though we were going to church, neither of us had a strong relationship with the Lord, matter-of-fact, I was feeling that emptiness inside and desperately tried to figure out the missing link. There were days I thought it would be more beneficial for me to just "check out" than to continue on in the misery.

The only excitement that had a way of shaking me out of my numbness was at work where a number of the gentlemen I worked with often gave me flirtatious attention. Their suggestive comments and lingering looks made me feel alive again, desiring something I had longed for in my marriage.

Thankfully, God saw the train wreck ever before it began. After receiving a call about a job in the St. Louis area that paid a whole lot more money than we were used to, Rick and I drove up there – me at the interview, he looking around at area departments. I, unfortunately, did not get the job, but he was offered a position at Union Police Department by a God-fearing, Christian Chief.

Who would have thought that one phone call would change our lives for the better in just a matter of months?

Feeling the Lord directing our steps, we moved our family and headed north much to our parents' chagrin. It was the best thing that ever happened. Being on our own for that next year forced us to re-evaluate our marriage and our calling. The two of us began to mesh as a couple and we started laying the foundations of a rock-solid relationship.

Rick and I established ourselves in a good church and quickly got involved. I began classes at the local college and God initiated the process of opening doors for me to speak to women throughout the community and state.

Finally in 2008, after feeling a tug to write, I attended a Christian Writer's Conference where I was given the idea to write a devotional book for police wives. Voila. Just like that, the ministry was born.

The road was not easy and there were many frustrations, heartaches and closed doors along the way, but by 2010, I was traveling and speaking to numerous police wives' groups, and feeling the need to go further. I set up a website and called it Badge of Hope.

Though we weren't sure how it was going to look or what exactly God wanted us to do with it, we began to get the word out. More books, more invitations.

By 2013, I had developed a 3-hour seminar to focus on marriage, and I asked Rick to have a more active role in the presentation. With that, we have travelled from Canada to Texas to Maine and everything in between.

We've seen marriages on their last thread completely healed and people come to Christ. We've witnessed healing of mind and spirit for those burdened down by the weight of this world.

We've talked to those on the verge of ending their own life and heard the excitement of others in the infant stages of their career.

In August of 2014, we realized how much God had His hand on this ministry when the Ferguson riots broke out, and it seemed as if the whole nation was on the verge of combustion. God would use *us* and this trying situation for His good.

I wrote a blog that reached nearly a million hits. Most of the comments were positive and supportive, but many were hate-filled and antagonistic. I was interviewed on CNN, Larry Connors USA, Breitbart News and The Pathway. It was a nerve-wrecking time, but we saw God's amazing work throughout the whole ordeal.

One message I received from that incident will forever be engrained on my mind. An officer who had been on the frontlines day and night for a period of days as part of a SWAT unit, said he was sitting in his garage when he "happened" to run across my blog. "You'll never know the impact…never understand how you possibly saved a career."

Knowing how desperate these officers were during that time period, I'm sure he wasn't just referring to his career, but perhaps his life as well. I believe God stepped in and saved that officer as he sat there alone contemplating his future.

A couple months later, Badge of Hope was able to minister directly to the officers and Chief at Ferguson through a lunch we prepared, as well as through materials such as Bibles and books, and many prayers said over them.

Today as we look forward, we do not exactly know where this ministry will take us, but we do know that God is in control, He's the Great Healer of all, and without Him in our lives we can do nothing and are nothing.

-----

With that said, I want to encourage you today. If your marriage is falling apart or even if it is not, but is in a dormant state, know that it can be revived.

Wherever you are today in life, whether struggling with PTSD, feeling fatigued, overworked, or bogged down by the destructive actions of another, know that God is your source of strength. He alone can right the wrongs and bring healing within your soul, mind and spirit. He worked miracles in our life and can do the same with yours.


Blessings,

Kristi

# Bibliography

Brannan, T. (2001). *Domestic Violence in Police Families.* Retrieved from Purple Berets: http://www.purpleberets.org/violence_police_famili es.html

*Communication Skills.* (2008). Retrieved from Maximum Advantage: Psychology Applied to Life: http://www.maximumadvantage.com/communicatio n-skills/

Corcoran, K. (2014, July 4). *Undercover police officer suing the force after he became addicted to heroin during drugs operation.* Retrieved from Daily Mail: http://www.dailymail.co.uk/news/article-2680498/Undercover-GMP-officer-Robert-Carroll-suing-force-addicted-heroin-drugs-operation.html

*Domestic Violence in Police Families.* (2003). Retrieved from Purple Beret: http://www.purpleberets.org/violence_police_famili es.html

Dr. Jean G. Larned, P. (2010, Fall). Understanding Police Suicide. *Forensic Examiner Magazine.*

Fitzgerald, J. (2015, February 22). *Ex-New York Cop Glen Hochman, 2 Daughters Found Dead.* Retrieved from Huff Post Crime: http://www.huffingtonpost.com/2015/02/22/glen-hochman-cop-daughters-found-dead_n_6730136.html

*Former Connecticut police officer arrested 3 times in 11 hours on drunken-driving charges.* (2014, December 17). Retrieved from Fox News: http://www.foxnews.com/us/2014/12/17/former-connecticut-police-officer-arrested-3-times-in-11-hours-on-drunken/

Haines, S. C. (2003, September 19). *POLICE STRESS AND THE EFFECTS ON THE FAMILY.* Retrieved from E.M.U. SCHOOL OF POLICE STAFF AND COMMAND: http://www.emich.edu/cerns/downloads/papers/PoliceStaff/Shift%20Work%2C%20%20Stress%2C%20%20Wellness/Police%20Stress%20and%20the%20Effects%20on%20the%20Family.pdf

*Joshua Boren, Police Officer in Spanish Fork, UT, Kills 4 Family Members Then Himself.* (2014, January 17). Retrieved from Epoch Times: http://www.theepochtimes.com/n3/455573-joshua-boren-police-officer-in-spanish-fork-ut-kills-4-family-members-then-himself/

Matthews, R. (2011, Spring). *Law Enforcement Stress and Marriage.* Retrieved from (http://digitalcommons.liberty.edu/cgi/viewcontent.cgi?article=1218&context=honors)

Matthews, R. (2011, Spring). *Law Enforcement Stress and Marriage.* Retrieved from (http://digitalcommons.liberty.edu/cgi/viewcontent.cgi?article=1218&context=honors)

Michaels, R. (n.d.). *Serve & Protect.* Retrieved from Serve
& Protect: http://www.serveprotect.org

*Police Chiefs Discuss a Tough Issue...* (2012). Retrieved
from Subject to Debate:
http://www.policeforum.org/assets/docs/Subject_to
_Debate/Debate2012/debate_2012_sepoct.pdf

*Police Chiefs Discuss a Tough Issue: Alcohol and Drug
Abuse by Officers.* (2012). Retrieved from Subject
to Debate:
http://www.policeforum.org/assets/docs/Subject_to
_Debate/Debate2012/debate_2012_sepoct.pdf

Riley, S. (2012, February 10). *Cops and Addiction.*
Retrieved from Law Enforcement Today:
http://www.lawenforcementtoday.com/2012/02/10/c
ops-and-addiction/

Sam Torres, P. (2015, March). *Preparing Families for the
Hazards of Police Work.* Retrieved from The Police
Chief:
http://www.policechiefmagazine.org/magazine/inde
x.cfm?fuseaction=display_arch&article_id=120&iss
ue_id=102003

Stanton G. T. (2012, March). *The Christian Divorce Rate
Myth.* Retrieved from Crosswalk.com:
http://www.crosswalk.com/family/marriage/divorce-and-
remarriage/the-christian-divorce-rate-myth.html

# Additional Resources by the Author

*Standing Courageous,* 2011, Createspace, 160 pages

This book represents all voices of the law enforcement family, i.e. wives, parents, cousins, children, etc. The stories within will tear at your heart and bring laughter to your soul, but more importantly, offer a greater understanding and appreciation for the men and women who keep our homes and cities safe every day.

*Lives Behind the Badge,* 2009, Createspace, 158 pages

What wife of an officer hasn't lain awake at night wondering if her husband is safe, or has felt resentment when dinner once again grows cold all in the name of duty. In this book Kristi Neace brings forth real stories from LEO wives all over the country who have experienced similar issues such as: fear, anger, worry, respect, pride, thankfulness and much more. Each topic is inspired by a down-to-earth devotion reminding us that only through our Heavenly Father can we find peace in the midst of chaos; purpose in the eye of worldly indifference. Kristi covers the hot-button issues you're sure to face and gives you the tools to navigate in uncertain times.

*Layers: Living a Life Unhindered,* 2012, Createspace, 126 pages

What is holding you back from experiencing God in a spiritually intimate way? Do you desire to hear His voice and to understand His will for your life, but you feel as if your prayers aren't even reaching the ceiling? Then step into this study with Kristi as she travels through the layers we so often place between us and God. Things such as pride, anger, doubt, shame, self-reliance and unforgiveness. Just as an onion has many layers hiding away the fleshy heart of the bulb, we, too, allow layers to wrap around our hearts, hindering us from hearing His voice. So, what are you waiting for? We've got some peeling to do!

*Beyond the Blue,* 2013, Createspace, 64 pages

Jaralyn "Jari" Davison was just an ordinary housewife married to an extraordinary guy. Ted had always dreamed of being a police officer, but his love for those so-called "social outcasts" ran much deeper than even Jari could understand. After Ted was viciously gunned down in his squad car it would take many tears, much soul searching and a twist of fate to bring her to a point of forgiveness and, perhaps, an unconditional love for Ted's attacker. Her journey will leave you asking yourself, "How could someone offer forgiveness for such brutality and senselessness? Could I do the same or would I even be willing?" Just as Jari searched for those answers, sometimes our answers quietly come from beyond the blue.

*Between Friends: A Look at Mentoring God's Way,* 2006, Createspace, 92 pages

Join mentoring expert and author Kristi Neace as she explores the definition of a true godly mentor. In her warm, informal style, Kristi makes you will feel as though you are sitting in a quiet café, sipping coffee and chatting with a close friend. You will feel her passion for Women's Ministry and be challenged to make a difference in another woman's life through friendship. This three-week study not only is rich in Scripture but also covers the very basics of mentoring. Each day's thoughts and insight offer a complete picture of how a mentoring relationship was originally designed to be and offers practical solutions to bridge the gap between generations. Regardless of whether you are a women's ministry coordinator who would like to start a mentoring ministry in your church, a godly woman who would like to invest in a woman that needs some encouragement, or a young woman who could use some pointers from a more seasoned friend, this book will equip you and motivate you to jump right in to real, purposeful relationships.

# Badge of Hope Ministries

Badge of Hope Ministries is a Christian, non-denominational ministry to reach cops and their families for Christ, and to give them practical tools they can use in their everyday lives and marriages. We are constantly striving to make connections and network with other like-minded organizations to help further the kingdom.

For information about making a donation, visit
www.badgeofhopeministries.com

Donations are simple, fast and safe using PayPal, or can be mailed to our address at P.O. Box 113, Union, MO 63084.

Badge of Hope is a registered non-profit 501 (c) 3 designed as a public charity.

Made in the USA
Coppell, TX
02 April 2022